Worthy is the Lamb

PURITAN POETRY
IN HONOR OF THE SAVIOR

Material Compiled and Introductions
Written by
MAUREEN BRADLEY

⤙⤛⫯⤜⤚

Edited by
DR. DON KISTLER and JOEL RISHEL

SOLI DEO GLORIA PUBLICATIONS
...for instruction in righteousness...

SOLI DEO GLORIA PUBLICATIONS
A division of Soli Deo Gloria Ministries, Inc.

P. O. Box 451, Morgan PA 15064
(412) 221-1901 • Fax (412) 221-1902
www.SDGbooks.com

ISBN 1-57358-159-3

Biblical quotations found in the introductions are from the
New King James Version (NKJV)
© 1982 by Thomas Nelson.

Library of Congress Cataloging-in-Publication Data

Worthy is the lamb: Puritan poetry in honor of the Savior / material compiled and introductions written by Maureen Bradley ; edited by Don Kistler and Joel Rishel.
    p. cm.
    Includes index.
    ISBN 1-57358-159-3 (alk. paper)
    1. Christian poetry, English. 2. Jesus Christ—Poetry. 3. Christian poetry, American. 4. English poetry—Puritan authors. 5. American poetry—Puritan authors. 6. Puritan movements—Poetry. 7. Puritans—Poetry. I. Bradley, Maureen L., 1948- II. Kistler, Don. III. Rishel, Joel. IV. Title.

PR1195.J4W67 2004
821.008'03823–dc22

2004003972

Contents

Introduction

We do well to go to the giants of the Christian faith, the Puritans, for theologically substantial poetry. As with a multifaceted, sparkling diamond, their understanding of God is expressed from many unique and beautiful vantage points.

Perhaps their view of loving God more for what He is than for what He bestows, as Thomas Watson put it, is a neglected perspective in our day. For "True love is not mercenary. You need not hire a mother to love her child: a soul deeply in love with God needs not be hired by rewards" (Thomas Watson. *All Things for Good.* Edinburgh: Banner of Truth, 1991, p. 68.) Indeed, we would question the genuineness of a suitor's love who dated another only for how much he or she could benefit from the relationship, whether it was money, status in the community, physical gratification, or the like. Pure love is never characterized by self-interest (1 Corinthians 13). And if this is the standard for human relationships, must it not be applied to our relationship with God as well?

One glimpse of God, whose glory is the amazement of heaven, and our hearts are held captive as a mother who holds her baby for the first time. Once the eyes of the soul have come close to God, once you have been enabled to see yourself for what you are and God for who He is, it will be impossible to forget Him or turn back from Him. If the spiritual eyes of the soul have been opened by the Holy Spirit, the Pursuer of your soul will now be the Pursued. A soul deeply in love with God will not love the gifts He bestows only and forget to love the Giver of those gifts. Augustine said you must love God for Himself, His person, and His intrinsic excellencies.

May God enable us to step into the higher motive of seeking God for the sake of His own worth and loveliness; for it is the constant gazing upon His beauty that will keep the Christian joyfully walking toward the Celestial City to spend eternity with the Lover of his soul.

Obedience to God's clear instruction to "grow in the grace and knowledge" is fundamental to our spiritual well-being. However, our constant prayer should be that the Holy Spirit would enable us to be "a free and a voluntary people, and not compelled unto Christ…otherwise than by the sweet constraint of love" (Richard Sibbes. *Light from Heaven*. Ann Arbor: Sovereign Grace Publishers, 1961, p. 55).

In writing sacred poetry, the Puritans' desire was that "if the good spirit of God shine upon us at the time…[these poems] will be conducive to spiritualize the heart, wing the affections to heaven, and give us a blessed foretaste of the employment and felicity of elect angels, and of elect souls" (*The Works of the Rev. A. M. Toplady*, London: Ebenezer Palmer 1828, III:455).

Since the days of the Puritans, few authors have been able to show the majesty of God, the plague of the human heart, and the loveliness of Christ with the experiential depth of these spiritual giants. May the poetry in this book be an aid in our journey and help wing our affections to heaven.

As you finish reading these sacred poems, may you join Christian from John Bunyan's immortal *Pilgrim's Progress* in exclaiming, as he left Interpreter's house:

> *Here I have seen things rare and profitable,*
> *Things pleasant, dreadful, things to make me stable*
> *In what I have begun to take in hand;*
> *Then let me think on them, and understand.…*

Maureen Bradley
Richmond, IN

Worthy is the Lamb

The Song of the Angels and Church Together

RALPH ERSKINE

Come, let us join our cheerful songs with angels round the throne;
Ten thousand thousand are their tongues, but all their joys are one.

"Worthy's the Lamb that died," they cry, "O be exalted thus;
"Worthy's the Lamb," our lips reply, "for He was slain for us."

He's worthy to receive all pow'r, and riches all beside,
Wisdom, and strength, and honor, glory, and blessings on His head.

Power and dominion are His due, though doomed at Pilate's bar;
Wisdom belongs to Jesus too, tho' charged with madness here.

All riches are His native right, who bore amazing loss:
To Him belongs eternal might, who felt the weak'ning cross.

To Him be lasting honors paid instead of shame and scorn,
While glory shines around His head, a crown without a thorn.

He bore the curse for man that fell, to Him be blessings given:
The Lamb that sap'd the gate of hell hath gained the praise of heaven.

Thus angels crown their Lord, you see; more sib to Him may sing:
"Worthy's the Lamb, our kin, to be our Prophet, Priest, and King."

Erskine, Ralph. *Erskine's Sermons and Practical Works.*
Aberdeen: A. King & Co., 1863, VII:625-626.

His Glorious Estate

GOD THE CREATOR

The earth is the Lord's, and all its fullness,
The world and those who dwell therein.
For He has founded it upon the seas,
And established it upon the waters.

— PSALM 24:1-2

His Glorious Estate
GOD THE CREATOR

God is the creator of the world and all that is in it; therefore He is the owner of all by virtue of that fact. This truth the atheist refuses to accept. He sees himself as self-sufficient and attributes all of life to natural, impersonal processes alone. Cornelius Van Til addresses this worldview as follows: "Not believing in God you do not think yourself to be God's creature. And not believing in God you do not think the universe has been created by God. That is to say, you think of yourself and the world as just being there. Now if you actually are God's creature, then your present attitude is very unfair to Him. In that case it is even an insult to Him. And having insulted God, His displeasure rests upon you. God and you are not on 'speaking terms.' And you have very good reasons for trying to prove that He does not exist. If He does exist, He will punish you for your disregard of Him. You are therefore wearing colored glasses. And this determines everything you say about the facts and reasons for not believing in Him. You have, as it were, entered God's estate and have had your picnics and hunting parties there without asking His permission. You have taken the grapes of God's vineyard without paying Him any rent and you have insulted His representatives who asked you for it." (Van Til, Cornelius. *Why I Believe in God*. The Presbyterian and Reformed Publishing Company, Phillipsburg, NJ, n.d., pp. 11-12.)

While such a man has insulted God and His displeasure rests upon him, let us consider how seldom do even Christians stop to consider God's kindness to them. We breathe His air, walk on His ground, and eat the food from His gardens frequently without the least bit of thankfulness. By this careless attitude of ingratitude in our day to day lives we act as if we are totally autonomous. Even worse, we often malign and mistreat fellow human beings, as if they were ours to mistreat, disregarding God's mark of ownership on them (made in God's image). Our arrogance and ingratitude are a double insult for we do it having knowledge from Scripture and the Holy Spirit of these truths.

Children of the living God, stop a moment; open your eyes to the glorious estate on which God is allowing you to picnic. Give thanks to Him for His generosity to you here and for the magnificent estate He is preparing for you in eternity.

A Song of Praise to God

SAMUEL STENNETT

To God the universal King,
Let all mankind their tribute bring;
All that have breath, your voices raise,
In songs of never-ceasing praise.

The spacious earth on which we tread,
And wider heavens stretched o'er our head,
A large and solemn temple frame
To celebrate its builder's fame.

Here the bright sun that rules the day,
As through the sky he makes his way,
To all the world proclaims aloud
The boundless sovereignty of God.

When from his courts the sun retires,
And with the day his voice expires,
The moon and stars adopt the song,
And through the night the praise prolong.

The listening earth with rapture hears
The harmonious music of the spheres;
And all her tribes the notes repeat,
That God is wise, and good, and great.

But man, endowed with nobler powers,
His God in nobler strains adores;
His is the gift to know the song,
As well as sing with tuneful tongue.

Stennett, Samuel. *The Works of Samuel Stennett, D.D.*
London: Printed for Thomas Tegg, 1824, p. 531.

The Lord's People His Portion

PHILIP DODDRIDGE

Sovereign of nature, all is Thine,
The air, the earth, the sea;
By Thee the orbs celestial shine,
And cherubs live by Thee.

Rich in Thy own essential store,
Thou callest forth worlds at will;
Ten thousand, and ten thousand more,
Would hear Thy summons still.

What treasure wilt Thou then confess?
And Thy own portion call?
What by peculiar right possess,
Imperial Lord of all?

Thine Israel Thou wilt stoop to claim,
Wilt mark them out for Thine;
Ten thousand praises to Thy name
For goodness so divine!

That I am Thine, my soul would boast,
And boast its claim to Thee;
Nor shall God's property be lost,
Nor God be torn from me.

Doddridge, Philip. *The Miscellaneous Works of Philip Doddridge.*
London: Joseph Ogle Robinson, 1830, p. 984.

The Heavens Declare the Glory of God

AUGUSTUS TOPLADY

The sky's a veil, the outward scene
Proclaims the majesty within;
Which boundless light, though hid behind,
Breaks out, too great to be confined.

The heaven, Thy glorious impress wears,
Thy image glitters in the stars;
The firmament, Thine high abode,
Seems, too, the spangled robe of God.

Whene'er its beauty I admire,
Its radiant globes direct me higher,
In silent praise they point to Thee,
All light, all eye, all majesty!

Glory to Him who studs the sky,
Earth's variegated canopy,
With lamps to guide us on our way,
Faint emblems of eternal day.

Yes, Lord, each shining orb declares
Thy name in dazzling characters;
As precious gems they dart their rays
And seem to form a crown of praise.

Toplady, Augustus. *The Works of Augustus Toplady*,
J. Chidley, London: 1837, p. 895.

The God of Tempest and Earthquake

MATHER BYLES

Thy dreadful pow'r, Almighty God,
Thy works to speak conspire;
This earth declares Thy fame abroad,
With water, air, and fire.

At Thy command, in glaring streaks,
Thy ruddy lightning flies;
Loud thunder the creation shakes,
And rapid tempests rise.

Now gathering glooms obscure the day,
And shed a solemn night;
And now the heav'nly engines play,
And shoot devouring light.

The attending sea Thy will performs,
Waves tumble to the shore,
And toss, and foam amid the storms,
And dash, and rage, and roar.

The earth and all the trembling hills,
Thy marching footsteps own;
A shuddering fear her entrails fills,
Her hideous caverns groan.

My God, when terror thickest throng,
Through all the mighty space,
And rattling thunders roar along,
And bloody lightning blaze.

When wild confusion wrecks the air,
And tempests rend the skies,
While blended ruin, clouds and fire
In harsh disorder rise.

Amid the hurricane I'll stand
And strike a tuneful song;
My harp all trembling in my hand,
And all inspired my tongue.

I'll shout aloud, "Ye thunders, roll,
And shake the sullen sky;
Your sounding voice from pole to pole
In angry murmurs try."

Thou sun, retire, refuse thy light,
And let thy beams decay;
Ye lightnings, flash along the night,
And dart a dreadful day.

Let the earth totter on her base,
Clouds heavens wide arch deform;
Blow, all ye winds, from every place,
And breathe the final storm.

O Jesus, haste the glorious day,
When Thou shalt come in flame,
And burn the earth, and waste the sea,
And brake all nature's frame.

Come quickly, blessed hope, appear,
Bid Thy swift chariot fly;
Let angels warn Thy coming near,
And snatch me to the sky.

Around Thy wheels, in the glad throng,
I'd bear a joyful part;
All hallelujah on my tongue,
All rapture in my heart.

Byles, Mather. *Mather Byles' Works.*
Delmar: Scholars' Facsimiles & Reprints, 1978, pp. 7-8.

Proofs of God's Power and Wisdom in the Creation and Preservation of the World

RALPH ERSKINE

The Lord Jehovah built the skies,
And reared this stately frame;
The wide creation testifies
The greatness of His name.

The liquid element below
Was gathered by His hand;
The rolling seas together flow,
And leave the solid land.

To Him, the Maker, does pertain
What in the ocean is;
The finny people of the main,
And monsters there, are His.

The dusky shades of hell that lie,
Wrapped up in webs of night.
May well elude the solar eye,
But not th'Almighty's sight.

Death and destruction do in vain,
Their sable covering spread,
And in their secret vaults enchain,
Or fast lock up the dead.

The eye of the Almighty does
Their spoils entire survey;
And no distinction ever knows
Between the night and day.

He, o'er the airy empty place,
In pomp displays on high
The wide expanse, and ample space,
Of all the northern sky.

The ponderous earth, at His command,
Hangs in the ambient air;
No pillars bear the fabric grand,
But just His will and care.

He bids the clouds with water pent,
Imprisoned tempests chain;
Then their big floating wombs, unrent,
Suspend the birth of rain.

Again He bids their bosom ope,
And down the blessing pours,
To feed the lab'ring farmer's hope
With warm prolific show'rs.

Lest His high throne, so dazzling bright,
By naked eyes unseen,
With too much glory oppress our sight,
He spreads His clouds between.

He raises rocky fences round
The spacious swelling deep,
Which do the raging billows bound,
Mad waves in prison keep.

That while the rule of day and night,
The sun and moon maintain,
The rolling seas may have no might
To drown the earth again.

High hills that pillars seem and props
Of heaven's expanded roof,
Do quake, and bow their towering tops
Aghast at His reproof.

He cleaves the main, bids billows rise,
Then curbs the swelling tide;
How soon they cope with clouds and skies,
So soon He lays their pride.

The trembling waves at His command,
Creep softly to the shore;
Storms over-awed do silent stand,
Do quickly cease to roar.

Thus lawless seas He does control,
Diversifies the deep;
He makes the sleeping billows roll,
The rolling billows sleep.

He spreads the heavens, their azure face
He garnished by His might;
And did them most profusely grace
With constellations bright.

His hand the crooked serpent made;
But who can speak his art?
Of whom all's nothing that is said,
We know so small a part.

Who can the utmost force explore
Of His almighty hands?
For even the thunder of His pow'r
What mortal understands?

Erskine, Ralph. *Erskine's Sermons and Practical Works. Vol. 7.*
Aberdeen: A. King & Co., 1863, pp. 467-468.

The Friend Who Asked What God Is

AUGUSTUS TOPLADY

Is there a man whose daring hand
Can number every grain of sand?
Can count the drops that fill the sea,
Or tell how many stars that be?
Who, then, shall strive to comprehend
Infinity that knows no end?
Who shall set bounds to boundless power

Restrain omnipotence, or lower
Eternity to one poor hour?
Believe me, friend, thou canst no more
The vast designs of God explore,
Than thy short arm can touch the skies,
Or fathom ocean's deep abyss.
Who shall disclose his Maker's plan,

Or dare His secret will to scan?
Shall feeble, guilty, finite man?
None but perfection, such as His,
Can know th'Almighty as He is;
His glory never can be brought
Adapted to a mortal's thought.
Consider where thou art, and fear

This unseen witness always near.
Dive not into His deep decree,
The object's too elate for thee;
Thou must not ask, nor wish to see.
Cast each presumptuous doubt away;
Remember thou art, at best, but clay,
Whose only province is t'obey.

Toplady, Augustus. *The Works of Augustus Toplady,*
J. Chidley, London, 1837, p. 905

Ever Hallowed Be Thy Name

FRANCIS QUARLES

Nothing that e'er was made, was made for nothing—
Beasts for thy food, their skins were for thy clothing,
Flowers for thy smell, and herbs for curer good,
Trees for thy shade, their fruit for pleasing good,

The grass springs forth for beasts to feed upon,
And beasts are food for man; but man alone
Is made to serve his Lord in all his ways,
And be the trumpet of his Maker's praise.

Let heaven be then to me obdure as brass,
The earth as iron, inept for grain or grass;
Then let my flocks consume and never steed me,
Let pinching famine want wherewith to feed me,

When I forget to honor Thee, my Lord,
Thy glorious attributes, Thy works, Thy Word;
Oh, let the trump of Thine eternal fame,
Sound ever, ever hallowed be Thy name.

Quarles, Francis. *The Complete Works in Prose and Verse of Francis Quarles.* Lancashire: St. George's, Blackburn, 1880, II:28.

Almighty God

MATTHEW HALE

Almighty God, when He had raised the frame
Of heaven and earth, and furnished the same
With works of equal wonder, framed then
A piece of greater excellence, called "man."

Gave him a comprehensive soul, that soared
Above the creatures, and beheld his Lord;
Inscribed him with His image, and did fill
The compass of his intellect and will,

With truth and good; gave him the custody
Of His own bliss and immortality.
And justly now his Sovereign might demand
Subjection and obedience at his hand.

Were only being given, 'twere but right
His debt of duty should be infinite.
But here was more, a super-added dress
Of life, perfection, and happiness.

Yet this great King, for an experiment
Of man's deserved allegiance, is content
To use an easy precept, such as stood
Both with His creature's duty and his good.

Forbids one fruit on pain of death, and gives
Freely the rest, which he might eat and live.
But man rebels, and for one taste doth choose
His life, his God, his innocence to lose.

And now death-stricken, like a wounded deer,
Strictly pursued by guilt, and shame, and fear,
He seeks to lose himself; from God he flies,
And takes a wilderness of miseries.

A land of new transgression, where his curse
Is closer bound, his nature growing worse.
And while in this condition mankind lay,
A man should think his injured God should say,

"There lies accursed man, and let him lie
Entangled in that web of misery
Which his own sin has spun! I must be true
And just; unthankful man, thou hast thy due."

But 'twas not so. Though man the mastery
With his Creator's power and will dares try,
And being over-matched with power, disdains
To seek a pardon from his Sovereign.

The great and glorious God, the mighty King
Of heaven and earth, despised by such a thing
As man, a worm of his own making, breaks
The rules of greatness, and His creature seeks,

His froward creature—not in such a way
As once He did in the cool of that day
Wherein man sinned, and hid—such majesty
Had been too great for man's necessity.

But the eternal Son of God, the Word,
By which all things were made, the mighty Lord,
Assumes our flesh, and under that He lays,
And hides His greatness, and those glorious rays

Of majesty, which had been over bright,
And too resplendent for poor mortal's sight;
And under this disguise, the King of kings,
The message of His Father's mercy brings.

Solicits man's return; and pays the price
Of his transgression by the sacrifice
Of His own soul; and undertakes to cure
Their sin, their peace and pardon to procure.

To conquer death for him, and more than this,
To settle him in everlasting bliss.
And now, O man, could this excess of love
Thy thankfulness to such a height improve,

That it could fire thy soul into one flame
Of love, to only Him that bought the same,
At such a rate, yet still it were too small
To recompense thy Savior's love withal.

Once did He give thee being from the dust,
And for that only being, 'twere but just
To pay thy utmost self; but when once more
Thy being and thy bliss He did restore

By such a means as this, it doth bereave
Thy soul of hopes of recompense, and leaves
Thy soul insolvent. Twice to Him this day
Thou owest thyself, yet but one self can pay.

Hale, Matthew. *Contemplations, Moral and Divine.*
London: Sherwood, Neely, & Jones, n.d., II:580-583.

A Song of Praise for Creation

JOHN MASON

Thou wast, O God, and Thou wast blessed
Before the world began;
Of Thine eternity possessed,
Before time's glass did run.

Thou needest none Thy praise to sing
As if Thy joy could fade;
Couldst Thou have needed anything
That couldst have nothing made.

Great and good God, it pleased Thee
Thy Godhead to declare,
And what Thy goodness did prepare.

Thou spoke, and heaven and earth appeared,
And answered to Thy call;
As if their Maker's voice they heard,
Which is the creature's all.

Thou spoke the word, most mighty Lord,
Thy word went forth with speed;
Thy will, O Lord, it was Thy word,
Thy word it was Thy deed.

Thou brought forth Adam from the ground,
And Eve out of his side;
Thy blessing made the earth abound
With these two multiplied.

Those three great leaves—heaven, sea, and land—
Thy name in figures show,
Brutes feel the bounty of Thy hand,
But I my Maker know.

Should not I here Thy servant be,
Whose creatures serve me here?
My Lord, whom should I fear but Thee,
Who am Thy creatures' fear?

To whom, Lord, should I sing but Thee,
The Maker of my tongue?
Lo, other lords would seize on me,
But I to Thee belong.

As waters haste unto their sea,
And earth unto its earth;
So let my soul return to Thee,
From whom it had its birth.

But, ah! I'm fallen in the night,
And cannot come to Thee;
Yet speak the Word, let there be light,
It shall enlighten me.

And let Thy Word, most mighty Lord,
Thy fallen creature raise;
Oh make me o'er again, and I
Shall sing my Maker's praise.

Mason, John. *Spiritual Songs, or Songs of Praise to Almighty God.*
Edinburgh: James Taylor, 1880, pp. 26-28.

Praise to God from All Creatures

ISAAC WATTS

The glories of my Maker God
My joyful voice shall sing,
And call the nations to adore
Their Former and their King.

'Twas His right hand that shaped our clay,
And wrought this human frame;
But from His own immediate breath
Our nobler spirits came.

We bring our mortal pow'rs to God,
And worship with our tongues;
We claim some kindred with the skies,
And join th'angelic songs.

Let grovelling beasts of every shape,
And fowls of every wing,
And rocks, and trees, and fires, and seas,
Their various tributes bring.

Ye planets, to His honor shine,
And wheels of nature roll,
Praise Him in your unwearied course
Around the steady pole.

The brightness of our Maker's name
The wide creation fills,
And His unbounded grandeur flies
Beyond the heavenly hills.

Watts, Isaac. *The Psalms and Hymns of Isaac Watts.*
Morgan: Soli Deo Gloria Publications, 1997, pp. 453-454.

The Glory of God in Christ

RALPH ERSKINE

All nature spreads, with open blaze,
Her Maker's name abroad;
And every work of His displays
The power and skill of God.

But in the grace that rescued man,
His brightest glory shines;
Here on the cross 'tis fairest drawn,
In precious bloody lines.

Here His whole name appears complete;
And who can guess or prove,
Which of the letters best are writ,
The wisdom, power, or love?

Justice and mercy, truth and grace,
In all their sweetest charms,
Here met, and joined their kind embrace,
With everlasting arms.

Erskine, Ralph. *Erskine's Sermons and Practical Works.*
Aberdeen: A. King & Co., 1863, VII:610.

A Song of Praise for the Patience of God

JOHN MASON

Almighty God, how hast Thou borne
Wrongs not to be expressed—
Daring rebellion, injured love,
Light quenched in my breast?
Man would be God, and down he fell,
Yet he lifts up his bruised bones
Against his Maker still.

Lord, what a monster is base man,
Thus given to rebel!
Oh, that Thou dost not cleave the earth,
And send him quick to hell!
His sins for wages loudly cry;
Justice, with dreadful sound,
Cries too, cut down this fruitless tree,
Why cumbers it the ground?

But God waves His advantages
Of right and vengeance too;
And by His single patience
Doth daring man outdo.
The creature doth disdain his God,
By whom he is maintained;
Yet God maintains this rebel worm
By whom He is disdained.

Fool, ask not where the Almighty is;
All glory to Him give;
Is not His power most fully proved
In suffering thee to live?
Were He not God, He could not bear
Such weights as on Him lie;
Weak things are quickly set on fire,
And to their weapons fly.

Why should not patience make me sing,
When hell would make me roar?
Lord, let Thy patience end in love,
I'll sing forevermore.

Mason, John. *Spiritual Songs, or Songs of Praise to Almighty God.*
Edinburgh: James Taylor, 1880, pp. 68-69.

A Foreign Fair Flower

SINFULNESS OF MAN

Holiness is a flower that grows not in nature's garden.
Men are not born with holiness in their hearts,
As they are born with tongues in their mouths:
Holiness is of a Divine offspring:
It is a pearl of price that is to be found in no nature
but a renewed nature, in no bosom but a sanctified bosom.
There is not the least beam or spark of holiness in any
natural man in the world.

— THOMAS BROOKS

A Foreign Fair Flower
SINFULNESS OF MAN

Nature's garden grows many weeds in the human heart, but not a single pure, white flower. When the Divine Gardener comes to plant His fair seed, He finds a very unsuitable garden plot indeed.

Long ago in the beginning this had been a lovely place with birds singing, beautiful, delicate blossoms blooming, and the Son shining. However, another sly, shiftless, tenant farmer (Satan) came and sowed the seeds of doubt, envy, and pride. Now the whole garden has been taken over by ugly weeds of various sorts. Thriving now are weeds of selfishness, weeds of covetousness, weeds of anger and hate, weeds of unbelief, weeds of deceitfulness, and weeds of pride.

Fallen creatures are by nature strangers and enemies to holiness, by nature have a bent toward sin and hell, and by nature turn their backs against God and holiness. What a despicable plot of ground is every human heart.

The divine Gardener does not despair, but sets to work. New soil is brought in by the regenerating work of the Holy Spirit. He prepares the ground and turns the sod by convictions of sin. He plants the seed of faith in Christ's justifying cross work. The tender plant sprouts and it is carefully nurtured by this expert Horticulturist. He fertilizes it with the Word, the Son shines on it causing growth, and it is watered by streams of mercy from His own river (Psalm 46:4).

Our God is diligent not to neglect the little garden, for weeds still sprout; thus it needs continual weeding by confession of sin. It is a relentless task to cultivate, subdue, and keep obedient the human heart, making it suitable to grow that which is "fair as is the rose in May." However, one day in glory this flower will be full grown and perfect. It will be presented, along with other blossoms, as a beautiful bouquet to the Father who will display His glorious work of redemption to all of the universe.

Adam

JOHN NEWTON

On man, in His own image made,
How much did God bestow!
The whole creation homage paid,
And owned him lord below.

He dwelt in Eden's garden, stored
With sweets for every sense;
And there, with his descending Lord,
He walked in confidence.

But, oh, by sin how quickly changed!
His honor forfeited,
His heart from God and truth estranged,
His conscience filled with dread!

Now from his Maker's voice he flees,
Which was before his joy,
And thinks to hide, amid the trees,
From an all-seeing eye.

Compelled to answer to his name,
With stubbornness and pride,
He cast on God Himself the blame,
Nor once for mercy cried.

But grace, unasked, his heart subdued,
And all his guilt forgave;
By faith the promised Seed he viewed,
And felt His pow'r to save.

Thus we ourselves would justify,
Though we the law transgress;
Like him, unable to deny,
Unwilling to confess.

But when, by faith, the sinner sees
A pardon, bought with blood,
Then he forsakes his foolish pleas,
And gladly turns to God.

Newton, John. *The Works of the Rev. John Newton.*
Edinburgh: Thomas Nelson, 1841, p. 525.

The Fall of Adam

RALPH ERSKINE

Old Adam once a heaven of pleasure found,
While he with perfect innocence was crowned.
His winged affections to his God could move
In raptures of desire, and strains of love.

Man standing spotless, pure, and innocent,
Could well the law of works with works content;
Though then, nor since, it could demand no less
Than personal and perfect righteousness!

These unto sinless men were easy terms,
Though now beyond the reach of withered arms.
The legal covenant then upon the field,
Perfection sought, man could perfection yield.

Rich had he and his progeny remained,
Had he primeval innocence maintained.
His life had been a rest without annoy,
A scene of bliss, a paradise of joy.

But subtle Satan, in the serpent hid,
Proposing fair the fruit that God forbid,
Man soon seduced by hell's alluring art,
Did, disobedient, from the rule depart,

Devoured the bait, and by his bold offence
Fell from his blissful state of innocence,
Prostrate, he lost his God, his life, his crown,
From all his glory tumbled headlong down,

Plunged in a deep abyss of sin and woe,
Where, void of heart to will, or hand to do;
For's own relief he can't command a thought,
The total sum of what he can is nought.

He's able only now to increase his thrall,
He can destroy himself, and this is all,
But can the hellish brat heav'n's law fulfill?
Whose precepts high surmount his strength and skill,

Can filthy dross produce a golden beam?
Or poisoned springs a salutif'rous stream?
Can carnal mind, fierce enmity's wide maw,
Be duly subject to the divine law?

Nay, now its direful threatenings must take place
On all the disobedient human race,
Who do by guilt Omnipotence provoke,
Obnoxious stand to His uplifted stroke.

They must engulf themselves in endless woes,
Who to the living God are deadly foes;
Who natively His holy will gainsay,
Must to His awful justice fall a prey.

In vain do mankind now expect, in vain
By legal deeds immortal life to gain;
Nay, death is threatened, threats must have their due,
Or souls that sin, must die; as God is true.

Erskine, Ralph. *Erskine's Sermons and Practical Works.*
Aberdeen: A. King & Co., 1863, VII:74-75.

Desiring to be Given up to God

AUGUSTUS TOPLADY

Oh, that my heart was right with Thee,
And loved Thee with a perfect love!
Oh, that my Lord would dwell in me,
And never from His seat remove!
Jesus, remove the impending load,
And set my soul on fire for God!

Thou seest I dwell in awful night
Until Thou in my heart appear;
Kindle the flame, O Lord, and light
Thine everlasting candle there.
Thy presence puts the shadows by;
If Thou art gone, How dark am I?

Ah, Lord, how should Thy servant see,
Unless Thou give me seeing eyes?
Well may I fall, if out of Thee;
If out of Thee, how should I rise?
I wander, Lord, without Thy aid,
And lose my way in midnight's shade.

Thy bright, unerring light afford,
A light that gives the sinner hope;
And from the house of bondage, Lord,
Oh, bring the weary captive up.
Thine hand alone can set me free,
And reach Thy pardon out to me.

Oh, let my prayer acceptance find,
And bring the mighty blessing down;
With eye-salve, Lord, anoint the blind,
And seal me Thine adopted son;
A fallen, helpless creature take,
And heir of Thy salvation make.

Toplady, Augustus. *The Works of Augustus Toplady, B.A.,*
London, 1837, p. 888

Self-Acquaintance

JOHN NEWTON

Dear Lord, accept a sinful heart,
Which of itself complains,
And mourns, with much and frequent smart,
The evil it contains.

There fiery seeds of anger lurk,
Which often hurt my frame;
And wait but for the tempter's work,
To fan them to a flame.

Legality holds out a bribe
To purchase life from Thee;
And discontent would fain prescribe
How Thou shalt deal with me.

While unbelief withstands Thy grace,
And puts Thy mercy by,
Presumption, with a brow of brass,
Says, "Give me, or I die."

How eager are my thoughts to roam
In quest of what they love;
But, ah, when duty calls them home,
How heavily they move!

Oh, cleanse me in a Savior's blood,
Transform me by Thy pow'r;
And make me Thy beloved abode,
And let me rove no more.

Newton, John. *The Works of the Rev. John Newton.*
Edinburgh: Thomas Nelson, 1841, p. 613.

His Wounds, Our Cure

MATTHEW HALE

The Prince of Darkness, flushed with vict'ry
In our first parents' first apostasy,
Usurped a lawless sovereignty on man,
Revolted thus from his first Sovereign.

And though by that apostasy he found,
Under the chains of death, his vassal bound,
Yet to secure his empire, he overspread
The world with darkness, and thereby did lead

His captives as he please. Thus he bears
His rule usurped near four thousand years;
Except some small confined plantation,
Within a family or nation.

But now to put a period to this reign
Of this usurper, and reduce again
Man to his just subjection, 'tis decreed
That man from this subjection shall be freed.

And this not by the absolute command
Of an immediate pow'r, nor shall the bands
Of angels, glorious hosts, engaged be
To rescue man from this captivity.

But God an unsuspected means intends,
And yet most suitable unto this end.
Sin stained our nature, and the serpent's wile
Did man of innocence and life beguile;

By man his head is crushed; the lawful Lord
Unto His creature man to his life restored;
A virgin's Son is born; this rising sun
The world's enthralling darkness overruns.

A Child to us is born, whose innocence
Our nature's spot and stain doth purge and cleanse;
His wounds, our cure; His bonds, our liberty;
His death becomes our life, our victory.

Hale, Matthew. *Contemplations, Moral and Divine.*
London: Sherwood, Neely, & Jones, n.d. II:592-593.

Original Sin

ISAAC WATTS

Backward with humble shame we look
On our original;
How is our nature dashed and broke
In our first father's fall!

To all that's good averse and blind,
But prone to all that's ill;
What dreadful darkness veils our mind!
How obstinate our will!

Conceived in sin, O wretched state,
Before we draw our breath;
The first young pulse begins to beat
Iniquity and death.

How strong in our degenerate blood
The old corruption reigns,
And, mingling with the crooked flood,
Wanders through all our veins.

Wild and unwholesome as the root
Will all the branches be;
How can we hope for living fruit
From such a deadly tree?

What mortal power from things unclean
Can pure productions bring?
Who can command a vital stream
From an infected spring?

Yet, mighty God! Thy wondrous love
Can make our nature clean,
While Christ and grace prevail above
The tempter, death, and sin.

The second Adam shall restore
The ruins of the first;
Hosanna to that sovereign power
That new-creates our dust!

Watts, Isaac. *The Psalms and Hymns of Isaac Watts.*
Morgan: Soli Deo Gloria Publications, 1997, p. 337.

Behold I Am Vile

JOHN NEWTON

O Lord, how vile am I,
Unholy and unclean!
How can I dare to venture nigh
With such a load of sin?

Is this polluted heart
A dwelling fit for Thee?
Swarming, alas, in every part,
What evils do I see!

If I attempt to pray,
And lisp Thy holy name,
My thoughts are hurried soon away,
I know not where I am.

If in Thy word I look,
Such darkness fills my mind;
I only read a sealed book,
But no relief can find.

Thy gospel oft I hear,
But hear it still in vain;
Without desire, or love, or fear,
I like a stone remain.

Myself can hardly bear
This wretched heart of mine;
How hateful, then, must it appear
To those pure eyes of Thine?

And must I then indeed
Sink in despair and die?
Fain would I hope that Thou didst bleed
For such a wretch as I.

That blood which Thou hast spilt,
That grace which is Thine own,
Can cleanse the vilest sinner's guilt,
And soften hearts of stone.

Low at Thy feet I bow,
Oh, pity and forgive;
Here will I lie, and wait till Thou
Shalt bid me rise and live.

Newton, John. *The Works of the Rev. John Newton.*
Edinburgh: Thomas Nelson, 1841, p. 607.

The Evil Heart

AUGUSTUS TOPLADY

Astonished and distressed,
I turn mine eyes within:
My heart with loads of guilt oppressed,
The seat of every sin.

What crowds of evil thoughts,
What vile affections there!
Distrust, presumption, artful guile,
Pride, envy, slavish fear.

Almighty King of saints,
These tyrant lusts subdue;
Expel the darkness of my mind,
And all my pow'rs renew.

This done, my cheerful voice
Shall loud hosannas raise;
My soul shall glow with gratitude,
My lips proclaim Thy praise.

Toplady, Augustus. *The Works of Augustus Toplady,*
J. Chidley, London, 1837, p. 909.

Self-Applause

JOHN NEWTON

My God, how perfect are Thy ways,
But mine polluted are;
Sin twines itself about my praise,
And slides into my prayer.

When I would speak what Thou hast done
To save me from my sin,
I cannot make Thy mercies known,
But self-applause creeps in.

Divine desire, that holy flame
Thy grace creates in me,
Alas, impatience is its name,
When it returns to Thee.

This heart a fountain of vile thoughts,
How does it overflow!
While self upon the surface floats,
Still bubbling from below.

Let others in the gaudy dress,
Of fancied merit shine,
The Lord shall be my righteousness,
The Lord forever mine.

Newton, John. *The Works of the Rev. John Newton.*
Edinburgh: Thomas Nelson, 1841, p. 547
("Jehovah Tsidkenu: The Lord Our Righteousness.").

A Most Gracious Design

GOD SOVEREIGN IN SALVATION

Who has saved us and called us with a holy calling,
Not according to our works,
But according to His own purpose and grace
Which was given to us in Christ Jesus
Before time began.

— 2 TIMOTHY 1:9

A Most Gracious Design
GOD SOVEREIGN IN SALVATION

The Scriptures reveal that our salvation begins in the love, grace, and mercy of the Father. Then both the Son and the Spirit each perform their proper part in carrying out the Father's electing love. In the fullness of time the Son accomplishes our redemption by His perfect life of obedience and His substitutionary atonement on the cross on behalf of His people. The Spirit then applies what Christ has accomplished to the elect chosen before the foundation of the world. This application results in a holy life lived (sanctification) by the enabling of the Spirit.

New England Puritan Thomas Shepard wrote, "The Father is glorious in His great work of election; the Son is glorious in His great work of redemption; the Holy Ghost is glorious in His work of application: The Father is glorious in choosing the house, the Son is glorious in buying the house, the Spirit is glorious in dwelling in the house." (Shepard, Thomas. *The Sincere Convert & Sound Believer.* Ligonier; PA: Soli Deo Gloria, 1991, p. 17.

Since each of us stood as a house which had been condemned, let us give thanks to the triune God for this glorious real estate transaction "to the praise of His glory."

The Harmony of Divine Perfections

SAMUEL STENNETT

When first the God of boundless grace
Disclosed His kind design;
To rescue our apostate race
From misery, shame, and sin.

Quick through the realms of light and bliss,
The joyful tidings ran;
Each heart exulted at the news,
That God would dwell with man.

Yet, 'midst their joys, they paused awhile,
And asked, with strong surprise,
But how can injured justice smile,
Or look with pitying eyes?

Will the Almighty deign again
To visit yonder world;
And hither bring rebellious men,
Whence rebels once were hurled?

Their tears, and groans, and deep distress,
Aloud for mercy call;
But, ah, must truth and righteousness
To mercy victims fall?

So spake the friends of God and man,
Delighted, yet surprised;
Eager to know the wondrous plan
That wisdom had devised.

The Son of God attentive heard,
And quickly thus replied,
"In Me let mercy be revered,
And justice satisfied.

"Behold, My vital blood I pour
A sacrifice to God;
Let angry justice now no more
Demand the sinner's blood."

He spake, and heav'n's high arches rung
With shouts of loud applause;
He died, the friendly angels sung,
Nor cease their rapturous joys.

Stennett, Samuel. *The Works of Samuel Stennett, D.D.*
London: Thomas Tegg, 1824, pp. 531–532.

The Method of Salvation

AUGUSTUS TOPLADY

The Father we bless,
Whose distinguishing grace,
Selected a people to show forth Thy praise;
Nor is Thy love known,
By election alone;
For, oh, Thou hast added the gift of Thy Son.

Thy goodness in vain
We attempt to explain,
Which found and accepted a ransom for men;
Great Surety of Thine,
Thou didst not decline
To concur with the Father's most gracious design.

To Jesus our Friend,
Our thanks shall ascend,
Who saves to the utmost, and loves to the end;
Our ransom He paid;
In His merit arrayed
We attain to the glory for which we were made.

Sweet Spirit of grace,
Thy mercy we bless,
For Thy eminent share in the council of peace;

Great agent divine,
To restore us is Thine,
And cause us afresh in Thy likeness to shine.

O God, 'tis Thy part,
To convince and convert,
To give a new life, and create a new heart;
By Thy presence and grace
We're upheld in our race,
And are kept in Thy love to the end of our days.

Father, Spirit, and Son,
Agree thus in One,
The salvation of those He has marked for His own;
Let us, too, agree
To glorify Thee,
Thou ineffable One, Thou adorable Three.

Toplady, Augustus. *The Works of Augustus Toplady.*
London: J. Chidley, 1837, p. 909.

Holy Three in One

JOHN NEWTON

Father of angels and of men,
Savior, who hast us bought,
Spirit by whom we're born again,
And sanctified and taught!

Thy glory, holy Three in One
Thy people's song shall be;
Long as the wheels of time shall run,
And to eternity.

Newton, John. *The Works of the Rev. John Newton.*
Edinburgh: Thomas Nelson, 1841, p. 634.

The Christian Scheme of Salvation Worthy of God

PHILIP DODDRIDGE

Immortal God, on Thee we call,
The great original of all;
Through Thee we are, to Thee we tend,
Our sure support, our glorious end.

We praise that wise mysterious grace,
That pitied our revolted race,
And Jesus, our victorious Head,
The Captain of salvation made.

He, Thine eternal love decreed,
Should many sons to glory lead;
And sinful worms to Him are given,
A colony to people heav'n.

Jesus for us—Oh, gracious name!—
Encounters agony and shame;
Jesus, the glorious and the great,
Was by dire suff'ring made complete.

A scene of wonders here we see,
Worthy the Son, and worthy Thee;
And while this theme employs our tongues,
All heaven unites its sweetest songs.

Doddridge, Philip. *The Miscellaneous Works of Philip Doddridge.*
London: Joseph Ogle Robinson, 1830, p. 1056-1057.

We Will Make Thee Borders of Gold, with Studs of Silver

RALPH ERSKINE

Object not, saying, "How shall I,
So weak, so black a swain,
Such beauties in Jehovah's eye
Or furnish or maintain?"

For with united power divine
We Father, Son, and Spirit,
Do stand engaged thee to refine,
And make thy form complete.

Keep thou no finite powers view,
To grace and deck thee thus;
Creation-work, both old and new,
Belongs to none but Us.

We'll make thee yet more radiant gems
Of grace, without thine aid,
To fence thy robe, like golden hems,
With silver studs inlaid.

Thy growing grace shall thrive and bear
A perfect crop at length;
Yet by no might within thy sphere,
But Our concurring strength.

Thy gold and silver ornament
Must strong and lasting prove;
For, lo, it is the pow'rful vent
Of Our eternal love.

Of old the good, the great Three-One,
Did jointly take thy part;
Thy naked soul We thought upon
With pity in Our heart.

We held a counsel for thy good,
Where I, without a sob,
Did choose a vesture dipped in blood
To buy thy golden robe.

Erskine, Ralph. *Erskine's Sermons and Practical Works.*
Aberdeen: A. King & Co., 1863, VII:320-321.

Election–Sovereign and Free

ISAAC WATTS

Behold the potter and the clay,
He forms His vessels as He please;
Such is our God, and such are we,
The subjects of His high decrees.

Doth not the workman's power extend
Over all the mass, which part to choose
And mold it for a nobler end,
And which to leave for viler use?

May not the sovereign Lord on high
Dispense His favors as He will,
Choose some to life, while others die,
And yet be just and gracious still?

What if, to make His terror known,
He lets His patience long endure,
Suff'ring vile rebels to go on,
And seal their own destruction sure?

What if He means to show His grace,
And His electing love employs
To mark out some of mortal race,
And form them fit for heav'nly joys?

Shall man reply against the Lord,
And call his Maker's ways unjust,
The thunder of whose dreadful word
Can crush a thousand worlds to dust?

But, O my soul, if truths so bright
Should dazzle and confound thy sight,
Yet still His written will obey,
And wait the great decisive day.

Then shall He make His justice known,
And the whole world before His throne
With joy or terror shall confess
The glory of His righteousness.

Watts, Isaac. *The Psalms and Hymns of Isaac Watts.*
Morgan: Soli Deo Gloria Publications, 1997, pp. 375-376.

The Covenant

JOHN NEWTON

The Lord proclaims His grace abroad!
Behold I change your hearts of stone;
Each shall renounce his idol-god,
And serve, henceforth, the Lord alone.

My grace, a flowing stream, proceeds
To wash your filthiness away;
You shall abhor your former deeds,
And learn My statues to obey.

My truth the great design ensures,
I give Myself away to you;
You shall be Mine, 1 will be yours,
Your God unalterably true.

Yet not unsought, or unimplored,
The plenteous grace shall I confer;
No—your whole heart shall seek the Lord,
I'll put a praying spirit there.

From the first breath of life divine,
Down to the last expiring hour,
The gracious work shall all be Mine,
Begun and ended in My pow'r.

Newton, John. *The Works of the Rev. John Newton.*
Edinburgh: Thomas Nelson, 1841, p. 548.

The Benefits Divine

AUGUSTUS TOPLADY

How vast the benefits divine,
Which we in Christ possess,
Saved from the guilt of sin we are,
And called to holiness.

But not for works which we have done,
Or shall hereafter do,
Hath God decreed on sinful worms
Salvation to bestow.

The glory, Lord, from first to last,
Is due to Thee alone;
Aught to ourselves we dare not take,
Or rob Thee of Thy crown.

Our glorious Surety undertook
To satisfy for man,
And grace was given us in Him,
Before the world began.

This is Thy will, that in Thy love
We ever should abide,
And lo, we earth and hell defy,
To make Thy counsel void.

Not one of all the chosen race,
But shall to heaven attain;
Partake on earth the purposed grace,
And then with Jesus reign.

Of Father, Son, and Spirit, we
Extol the three-fold care,
Whose love, whose merit, and whose pow'r
Unite to lift us there.

Toplady, Augustus. *The Works of Augustus Toplady,*
London: Printed for J. Chidley, 1837, p. 913.

Jesus

BENJAMIN KEACH

Look upon Me, and see My love descending;
'Tis from eternity, and has no ending.
Canst thou have more, O soul? Thou hast My heart,
Whatever is Mine, to thee I will impart.

Thy scarlet sins are washed quite away,
Nor one of them unto thy charge I'll lay.
Pull up thy drooping heart, be of good cheer,
Thy sins, though never so great, forgiven are.

I able am to save to the uttermost
All those who do put in Me all their trust.
These who do come to Me, I in no wise
Will cast them out; therefore lift up thine eyes;

Behold My hands and feet, and do not doubt,
For I have washed and cleansed thy soul throughout;
Thy debts I've paid, and quitted the old score,
Thy former faults I'll never remember more.

Cheer up thy heart, I tell thee, thou art Mine.
My blood was shed to save that life of thine.
With endless love thy soul I'll satisfy,
And in My bosom shalt thou ever lie.

In My unfolded arms I now thee take,
And do engage; I'll never thee forsake.
In sickness I'll be with thee until the end,
And death at last, I'll cause to be thy friend.

Making its final passage unto thee,
Only an entrance to felicity;
When with great glory thou shalt crowned be,
Seated forever on the throne with Me.

The world, death, nor the devil shall remove
My heart from thee; for those I truly love,
I love to the end; come, soul, and be
Blessed in My arms to all eternity.

Keach, Benjamin. *War with the Devil.*
London: Printed for E. Johnston, 1771, pp. 77-78.

The Frowardness of the Elect in the Work of Conversion

EDWARD TAYLOR

Those upon whom Almighty doth intend
His all eternal glory to expend,
Lulled in the lap of sinful nature snug,
Like pearls in puddles covered o'er with mud.

Whom, if you search, perhaps some few you'll find,
That to notorious sins were ne'er inclined;
Some shunning, some most, some great, some small,
Some this, that, or the other—some none at all.

But all, or almost all, you would easily find,
To all, or almost all, defects inclined;
To reel with the rabble rout who say,
"Let's hiss this piety out of our day."

And those whose frame is made of finer twine
Stand further off from grace than wash from wine.
Those who suck grace from the breast, are nigh as rare
As black swans that in milk-white rivers are.

Grace therefore calls them all, and sweetly woos.
Some will come in, the rest as yet refuse,
And run away; mercy pursues apace,
Then some cast down their arms, cry quarter, "Grace!"

Some chased out of breath, drop down with fear,
Perceiving the Pursuer drawing near.
The rest pursued, divide into two ranks,
And this way one, and that the other pranks.

Then in comes justice with her forces by her,
And doth pursue as hot as sparkling fire.
The right wing then begins to fly away:
But in the straights strong barricades lay.

They're therefore forced to face about, and have
Their spirits quelled, and therefore quarter crave.
These captived thus, justice pursues the game
With all her troops to take the other train.

Which being chased in a peninsula,
And followed close, they find no other way
To make escape, but to rally round about;
Which if it fail them that they get not out.

They're forced into the infernal gulf alive,
Or hacked in pieces are, or took captive;
But spying mercy stand with justice, they
Cast down their weapons, and for quarter pray.

Their lives are therefore spared, yet they are ta'ne
As the other band, and prisoners must remain.
And so they must now justice's captives be—
On mercies quarrel; mercy sets not free.

Their former captain is their deadly foe,
And now, poor souls, they know not what to do.

Taylor, Edward. *The Poetical Works of Edward Taylor.*
Princeton: Princeton University Press, 1943, pp. 46-47.

Behold and Wonder

MATTHEW HALE

Reader, behold and wonder! There was one
Obliged to his Prince, and Him alone
In all the bonds which duty, gratitude,
Or love could fasten; such as might exclude
All thoughts of a defection; yet this man
Breaks all; rebels against his Sovereign;
He flies, is apprehended, sentenced, cast,
And die he must; the final sentence passed
Knows no reversal. Lo, in that very now,
Wherein the offender waits his fatal blow,
The injured Lord doth substitute His own—
His own Son—into the prisoner's room,
Who takes the blow due to the traitor, dies,
The traitor's punishment to satisfy.
The case is mine and thine; by all the bands
Of nature, love and covenant, we stand
Engaged to Almighty God; we fell
From that allegiance when we did rebel
Against His law in Adam; by that law
We were condemned to die; no help we saw,
Or hope of rescue; then did His Majesty
Unveil that admirable mystery
Of our redemption; the Eternal Son
Of the Eternal God descends, becomes
Man for our sake, and in our stead doth stand,
And intercepteth from His Father's hand,
That stroke that was our due, becomes the price
Of our redemption and our sacrifice.

Hale, Matthew. *Contemplations, Moral and Divine,*
London: Sherwood, Neely, & Jones, n.d. II:594-595, "Poem upon Christmas Day," 1636.

The Principles of Christ's Doctrine

BENJAMIN KEACH

Repentance is wrought in my soul,
And faith for to believe;
Whereby on Jesus I do roll,
And truly Him receive,
As my dread Lord and Sovereign,
Him always to obey,
And in things over me to reign,
And govern every day.

Christ's baptism is very sweet,
With laying on of hands;
My soul is brought to Jesus' feet,
In owning His commands.
These ordinances men oppose,
And count as carnal things.
I have closed with, and hold to those,
From them rare comfort springs.

My precious Lord I must obey,
Though men reproach me still;
I'll do whatever Christ doth say,
And yield unto His will.
On Christ alone I do rely,
Though men judge otherwise;
Because I can't God's truth deny,
I am reproached with lies.

Let them deride, yet for Christ's sake,
Resolved now am I,
In His own strength the cross to take;
Yes, and for Him to die.
Because I'll ever turn my back
On Him whom I do love;
For I do know, I shall not lack
His presence from above.

For He has promised to the end,
To me He will be near;
And be to me a faithful friend,
Which makes me not to fear
Whatever men or devils do
In secret place design;
He soon can them quite overthrow,
And help this soul of mine.

The resurrection of the dead
I constantly maintain;
When all those which lie buried
Shall rise to life again,
And at the judgment day will come,
When Christ upon the throne,
Shall pass a black eternal doom
Upon each wicked one.

But all the saints then joyfully
With bowels He'll embrace,
And crowns to all eternity
Upon their heads will place.
And in Thy kingdom shall they reign,
Prepared long before,
And also shall with Christ remain
In bliss forevermore.

The sun doth now begin to shine,
And breaketh forth yet more and more;
Mere darkness was that light of mine,
Which I commended heretofore.
I was involved in my sin,
Had day without, but night within.

My former days I did compare
Unto the sweet and lovely spring;
I thought that time it was as rare,
As when the chirping birds do sing:
But I was blind, for now I see
There was no Spirit nor life in me.

My spring it was in winter time;
Yet like the midst of cold December,
The sun was gone out of my clime;
And also I do now remember,
My heart was cold as any stone,
My leaves were off, my sap was gone.

God is a sun, a shield also;
The glory of the world is He:
True light alone from Him doth flow,
And He has now enlightened me.
The sun doth His sweet beams display,
Like to the dawning of the day.

How precious it is to see the sun,
When in the morning it doth rise,
And shineth in our horizon,
To purify the clouded skies!
The misty fogs by His strong light
Are vanished quite out of sight.

Thus doth the Lord in my poor heart,
By His strong beams and glorious rays,
The light from darkness clearly part,
And make in me rare shining days:
Though fogs appear, and clouds do rise,
He doth expel them from mine eyes.

Were there no glorious lamp above,
What dark confusion would be there!
If God should quite the sun remove,
How would the seamen do to steer?
My soul's the world, and Christ's the sun;
If He shines not, I am undone.

In winter things hang down their head,
Until Sol's beams do them revive;
So I in sin lay buried,
Till Jesus Christ made me alive.

Alas, my heart was ice and snow,
Till sun did shine and winds did blow.

Until warm gales of heavenly wind
Did sweetly blow, and sun did dart
Its light in me, I could not find
No heart within my inward part.
Then blow thou wind, and shine thou sun,
To make my soul a lively one.

In natural men there is a light,
Which for their sins doth them reprove;
And yet they are but in the night,
And not renewed from above.
The moon is given—it is clear—
To guide men who in darkness are;

The sun for brightness doth exceed
The stars of heaven, or the moon;
Of them there is but little need,
When sun doth shine towards high noon;
Just so the gospel doth excel
The law God gave to Israel.

All those who do the gospel slight,
And rather have a legal guide,
The sun's not risen in their sight,
And therefore 'tis that they deride
Those who commend the gospel sun,
Above the light in every one.

Degrees of light they do perceive,
Some of them weak, and others strong;
That which is saving none receive,
But those unto whom Christ belong;
Yet doth each light serve for the end,
For which to man God did it send.

Keach, Benjamin. *War with the Devil.*
London: Printed for E. Johnston, 1771, pp. 91-95.

Fully Known and at Rest

SATISFACTION OF THE HEART

O Lord, You have searched me and known me.
You know my sitting down and my rising up;
You understand my thought afar off.
You comprehend my path and my lying down,
And are acquainted with all my ways.
For there is not a word on my tongue,
But behold, O Lord, You know it altogether.
You have hedged me behind and before,
And laid Your hand upon me.

— Psalm 139:1-5

Fully Known and at Rest
SATISFACTION OF THE HEART

"Ever since the days of St. Augustine, it has been a proverb that God has made the heart of man for Himself, and that the heart of man finds no true rest till it finds its rest in God. But long before the days of St. Augustine, the Psalmist had said the same thing. The heart of man, the Psalmist had said, is such that it can pour itself out nowhere but before God. In His sovereignty, in His wisdom, and in His love, God has made the heart of man so that at its *deepest*—but for Himself—it is absolutely solitary and alone. So much so that, 'Not even the tenderest heart, and next our own, knows half the reasons why we smile or sigh.' They see us smile, and they hear us sigh, but the reasons why we smile or why we sigh are fully known to God alone." (Whyte, Alexander. *Lord, Teach Us to Pray,* Grand Rapids: Baker Book House, 1976, p. 28.)

The need for a relationship, familiarity which includes love, honesty, safety, intimacy—this is part of our essence. Often we are led to believe that another human being can fulfill this need; perhaps in part, but not in full. God has reserved this resting place, this purity of familiarity for Himself alone. The reasons why we smile and sigh are not only understood but cherished by the triune God in whose image we are made.

In Psalm 62:8 God invites us to pour our hearts out before Him. Our sorrows surely will be lessened and our joys doubled as we accept His gracious invitation. And every time we step into the throne room of heaven for a private conversation with our tender, compassionate, all-wise Creator, may we marvel at God's extraordinary mercy and goodness to us in the redemption He has accomplished in the crosswork of Christ.

I Rest in Thee

AUGUSTUS TOPLADY

Oh, may I never rest,
Till I find my rest in Thee;
Till of my pardon here possessed,
I feel Thy love to me!
Unseal my darkened eyes,
My fettered feet unbind,
The lame shall, when Thou say, "Arise,"
Run swifter than the hind.

Oh, draw the alien near,
Bend the obdurate neck,
Oh, melt the flint into a tear,
And teach the dumb to speak;
Turn not Thy face away,
Thy look can make me clean;
Me in Thy wedding robe array,
And cover all my sin.

Tell me, my God, for whom
Thy precious blood was shed;
For sinners, Lord, as such I come,
For such the Saviour bled.
Then raise a fallen wretch,
Display Thy grace in me!
I am not out of mercy's reach,
Nor too far gone for Thee.

Thou quickly wilt forgive,
My Lord will not delay;
Jesus, to Thee the time I leave,
And wait the accepted day.
I now rejoice in hope.
That I shall be made clean;
Thy grace shall surely lift me up

Above the reach of sin.
Hast Thou not died for me,
And called me from below!
Oh, help me to lay hold on thee,
And never to let Thee go!
Though on the billows tossed,
My Savior I'll pursue;
Awhile submit to bear His cross,
Then share His glory too.

Toplady, Augustus. *The Works of Augustus Toplady, B.A.,*
London: Printed for J. Chidley, 1837, p. 889 (Poem XVII).

Invitation

GEORGE HERBERT

Turn in, my Lord, turn in to me;
My heart's a homely place;
But Thou canst make corruption flee,
And fill it with Thy grace;
So furnished it will be brave,
And a rich dwelling Thou shalt have.

It was Thy lodging once before,
It builded was by Thee;
But I to sin set op'n the door,
It rendered was by me.
And so Thy building was defaced,
And in Thy room another placed.

But he usurps, the right is Thine;
Oh, dispossess him, Lord.
Do thou but say, "This heart is Mine."
He's gone at the first word.
Thy word's Thy will, Thy will's Thy power,

Thy time is always; now's mine hour.
Now say to sin, "Depart;
And, son give me thine heart."
Thou, that by saying,
"Let it be," didst make it,
Canst, if Thou wilt, by saying,
"Give to Me," take it.

Herbert, George. *The Works of George Herbert in Prose and Verse.*
London: Bell and Dalby, 1859, II:353.

Communion with God

JOHN MASON

Alas, my God, that we should be
Such strangers to each other;
Oh, that as friends we might agree,
And walk and talk together.
Thou knowest my soul does dearly love
The place of Thine abode;
No music drops so sweet a sound,
As these two words—*My God.*

I long not for the fruit that grows
Within these gardens here;
I find no sweetness in their rose,
When Jesus is not near.
Thy gracious presence, O my Christ,
Can make a paradise;
Ah! what are all the goodly pearls
Unto this Pearl of Price?

May I taste that communion, Lord,
Thy people have with Thee?
Thy Spirit daily talks with them,
Oh, let Him talk with me.

Like Enoch, let me walk with God,
And thus walk out my day,
Attended by the heavenly guards
Upon my King's highway.

When wilt Thou come to me, O Lord?
Oh, come, my Lord most dear;
Come near, come nearer, nearer still,
I'm well when Thou art near.
When wilt Thou come to me, O Lord?
I languish for Thy sight,
Ten thousand suns, if Thou art strange,
Are shades instead of light.

When wilt Thou come to me, O Lord?
For till Thou dost appear,
I count each moment for a day,
Each minute for a year.
Come, Lord, and never from me go,
This world's a darksome place;
I find no pleasure here below,
When Thou dost veil Thy face.

There's no such thing as pleasure here,
My Jesus is my all;
As Thou dost shine or disappear,
My pleasures rise or fall.
Come, spread Thy savor o'er my frame;
No sweetness is so sweet,
Till I get up to sing Thy name,
Where all Thy singers meet.

Mason, John. *Spiritual Songs, or Songs of Praise to Almighty God.*
Edinburgh: James Taylor, 1880, pp. 161-163.

The God of Spirits Sought

PHILIP DODDRIDGE

Father of spirits, from Thy hand,
Our souls immortal came;
And still Thine energy divine
Supports th'ethereal flame.

By Thee our spirits all are known;
And each remotest thought
Lies wide expanded to His eye,
By whom their pow'rs were wrought.

To Thee, when mortal comforts fail,
Thy flock deserted flies;
And, on the eternal Shepherd's care,
Our cheerful hope relies.

When o'er Thy faithful servant's dust,
Thy dear assemblies mourn,
In speedy tokens of Thy grace,
O Israel's God, return.

The pow'rs of nature all are Thine,
And Thine the aids of grace;
Thine arm has borne Thy churches up
Through every rising race.

Exert Thy sacred influence here,
And here Thy suppliants bless,
And change, to strains of cheerful praise,
Their accents of distress.

With faithful heart, with skilful hand,
May this Thy flock be fed;
And with a steady growing pace,
To Zion's mountain led.

Doddridge, Philip. *Miscellaneous Works of Philip Doddridge.*
London: Joseph Robinson, 1830, p. 984.

Happiness Found

AUGUSTUS TOPLADY

Happiness, thou lovely name,
Where's thy seat, oh, tell me where?
Learning, pleasure, wealth, and fame,
All cry out, "It is not here."
Not the wisdom of the wise,
Can inform me where it lies;
Not the grandeur of the great,
Can the bliss I seek create.

Object of my first desire,
Jesus crucified for me!
All to happiness aspire,
Only to be found in Thee;
Thee to praise, and Thee to know,
Constitute our bless below;
Thee to see, and Thee to love,
Constitute our bliss above.

Lord, it is not life to live,
If Thy presence Thou deny;
Lord, if though Thy presence give,
'Tis no longer death to die.
Source and Giver of repose,
Singly from Thy smile it flows;
Peace and happiness are Thine;
Mine they are, if Thou art mine.

While I feel Thy love to me,
Every object teems with joy;
Here, oh, may I walk with Thee,
Then into Thy presence die!
Let me but Thyself possess,
Total sum of happiness!
Real bless I then shall prove,
Heav'n below and heav'n above.

Toplady, Augustus. *The Works of Augustus Toplady,*
London: Printed for J. Chidley, 1837, p. 909.

Rest for the Weary Soul

JOHN NEWTON

Does the gospel-word proclaim
Rest for those who weary be?
Then, my soul, put in thy claim,
Sure that promise speaks to thee.
Marks of grace I cannot show,
All polluted is my best;
Yet I weary am, I know,
And the weary long for rest.

Burdened with a load of sin,
Harassed with tormenting doubt,
Hourly conflicts from within,
Hourly crosses from without.
All my little strength is gone,
Sink I must without supply;
Sure upon the earth is none
Can more weary be than I.

In the ark the weary dove
Found a welcome resting place;
Thus my spirit longs to prove
Rest in Christ, the ark of grace.
Tempest-tossed I long have been,
And the flood increases fast;
Open, Lord, and take me in,
Till the storm be overpassed.

Safely lodged within Thy breast,
What a wondrous change I find!
Now I know Thy promised rest
Can compose a troubled mind.
You that weary are, like me,
Harken to the gospel-call;
To the ark for refuge flee,
Jesus will receive you all!

Newton, John. *The Works of the Rev. John Newton.*
Edinburgh: Thomas Nelson, 1841, p. 609.

The Comparison, the Choice, and the Enjoyment

MATHER BYLES

Who on the earth, or in the skies,
Thy beauties can declare?
Jesus, dear object of my eyes,
My everlasting fair.

Mortals, for you this is too great,
Too bright, and too sublime;
This angels labor to repeat,
And sink beneath the theme.

Behold, ye beauties here below,
And clasp Him in your arms:
Can ye such heavenly graces show,
Or rival Him in charms?

Though now, delighted, we can trace
Your colors as they lie,
When He appears, from off your face
The fading colors fly.

When all your charms in vain we seek,
And all your joys are fled,
Beauty blooms rosy on his cheek,
And dances round his head.

In vain your softest smiles appear,
Or lovely blushes rise;
Eternal transports center here,
Heaven brightens in these eyes.

Unveil, Almighty Love, Thy face,
Thy features let me see;
At once I'll rush to Thy embrace,
I'll spring at once to Thee.

Thus fixed forever—oh, the joys!
The unutterable bliss!
Now where's your pleasure, earthly toys,
Can ye compare with this?

No more from Thy embrace I'll roam,
My Lord, my life, my love,
I see the scenes of joys to come
In long procession move.

How, vast eternity, roll on,
Oh, fathomless profound!
Ye endless ages, swiftly run,
Your never-ceasing round.

Byles, Mather. *Mather Byles' Works.*
Delmar: Scholars' Facsimiles & Reprints, 1978, p. 21-23.

Fervent Desire

AUGUSTUS TOPLADY

Father, I want a thankful heart,
I want to taste how good Thou art.
To plunge me in Thy mercy's sea,
And comprehend Thy love to me—
The length, and depth, and breadth, and height
Of love divinely infinite.

Jesus, my great High Priest above,
My Friend before the throne of love!
If now for me prevails Thy prayer,
If now I find Thee pleading there,
Hear, and my weak petitions join,
Almighty Advocate, to Thine.

O sovereign Love, to Thee I cry,
Give me Thyself, or else I die;
Save me from death, from hell set free,
Death, hell, are but the want of Thee;
My life, my crown, my heaven Thou art!
Oh, may I find Thee in my heart!

Toplady, Augustus. *The Works of Augustus Toplady,*
London: J. Chidley, 1837, p. 914.

The Way of Access

JOHN NEWTON

One glance of Thine, eternal Lord,
Pierces all nature through;
Nor heaven, nor earth, nor hell afford
A shelter from Thy view.

The mighty whole, each smaller part,
At once before Thee lies;
And every thought of every heart
Is open to Thine eyes.

Though greatly from myself concealed,
Thou seest my inward frame;
To Thee I always stand revealed,
Exactly as I am.

Since, therefore, I can hardly bear
What in myself I see;
How vile and black must I appear,
Most holy God, to Thee?

But since my Savior stands between,
In garments dyed in blood,
'Tis He, instead of me, is seen,
When I approach to God.

Thus, though a sinner, I am safe;
He pleads before the throne,
His life and death in my behalf,
And calls my sins His own.

What wondrous love, what mysteries,
In this appointment shine!
My breaches of the law are His,
And His obedience mine.

Newton, John. *The Works of the Rev. John Newton.*
Edinburgh: Thomas Nelson, 1841, p. 617-618.

God My Only Happiness

ISAAC WATTS

My God, my portion, and my love,
My everlasting all!
I've none but Thee in heaven above,
Or on this earthly ball.

What empty things are all the skies,
And this inferior clod!
There's nothing here deserves my joys,
There's nothing like my God.

In vain the bright, the burning sun,
Scatters his feeble light;
'Tis Thy sweet beams create my noon;
If Thou withdraw, 'tis night.

And while upon my restless bed,
Among the shades I roll,
If my Redeemer shows His head,
'Tis morning with my soul.

To Thee we owe our wealth, and friends,
And health, and safe abode;
Thanks to Thy name for meaner things,
But they are not my God.

How vain a toy is glittering wealth,
If once compared to Thee!
Or what's my safety, or my health,
Or all my friends to me?

Were I possessor of the earth,
And called the stars my own,
Without Thy graces and Thyself
I were a wretch undone.

Let others stretch their arms like seas,
And grasp in all the shore;
Grant me the visits of Thy face,
And I desire no more.

Watts, Isaac. *The Psalms and Hymns of Isaac Watts.*
Morgan: Soli Deo Gloria Publications, 1997, pp. 470-471.

The Hidden Life

JOHN NEWTON

To tell the Saviour all my wants,
How pleasing is the task!
Nor less to praise Him when He grants
Beyond what I can ask.

My laboring spirit vainly seeks
To tell but half the joy;
With how much tenderness He speaks,
And helps me to reply.

Nor were it wise, nor should I choose,
Such secrets to declare;
Like precious wines, their taste they lose,
Exposed to open air.

But this, with boldness, I proclaim,
Nor care if thousands hear,
Sweet is the ointment of His name,
Not life is half so dear.

And can you frown, my former friends,
Who knew what once I was,
And blame the song that thus commends
The Man who bore the cross?

Trust me, I draw the likeness true,
And not as fancy paints;
Such honor may He give to you,
For such have all His saints.

Newton, John. *The Works of the Rev. John Newton.*
Edinburgh: Thomas Nelson, 1841, p. 619.

What Glories All Divine

(Based upon Psalm 84:11)

SAMUEL STENNETT

Great God, amid the darksome night,
Thy glories dart upon my sight,
While, wrapped in wonder, I behold
The silver moon and stars of gold.

But, when I see the sun arise,
And pour his glories o'er the skies,
In more stupendous forms I view
Thy greatness and Thy goodness too.

Thou Sun of suns, whose dazzling light,
Tries and confounds an angel's sight!
How shall I glance mine eye at Thee,
In all Thy vast immensity?

Yet I may be allowed to trace
The distant shadows of Thy face;
As, in the pale and sickly moon,
We trace the image of the sun.

In ev'ry work Thy hands have made,
Thy pow'r and wisdom are displayed;
But, oh, what glories all divine,
In my incarnate Savior shine!

He is my Sun; beneath His wings
My soul securely sits and sings;
And there enjoys, like those above,
The balmy influence of Thy love.

Oh, may the vital strength and heat,
His cheering beams communicate,
Enable me my course to run
With the same vigor as the sun!

Stennett, Samuel. *The Works of Samuel Stennett, D.D.*
London: Thomas Tegg, 1824, p. 541.

In Thee Alone I Must Be Blessed

SAMUEL DAVIES

No, never, never can this heart,
From Thee her God, her all, depart.
Indulge my boldness; I protest
In Thee alone I must be blessed;
I'm fixed, resolv'dly fixed, in this
Thyself, or nought shall be my bliss;
I swear by the eternal Three,
I will accept no bliss but Thee.
Put me not off with golden toys,
With empty honors, sensual joys.

Oh, do not Thy poor servant doom
To crowns and empires in Thy room.
I loath the happiness that springs
From these and all created things,
Sooner may gold or dust assuage
The parched pilgrim's thirsty rage,
When under torrid Lybian skies,
On burning sands, he faints and dies;
Sooner, than these inferior toys,
Can fill me with substantial joys.

Since of Thy love I tasted first,
All other pleasures I disgust.
Since first Thy beauties charmed my sight,
Created charms yield no delight.
Oh, if I'm doomed Thy frowns to feel,
Why didst Thou e'er Thy smiles reveal?
Why with Thy glories charm my eye,
If I must see and ne'er enjoy?
Oh, why torment me with the views
Of bliss I must forever lose?

Oh, if I must forever dwell
Absent from Thee, why did not hell
Devour me, e'er I felt this flame?
This ardent passion to Thy name?
Then had my soul ne'er understood
The loss of an infinite good;
Nor languished in eternal pain,
Pleasures once tasted to regain;
Nor in tormenting anguish pined
To call Thy once felt smiles to mind.

But hence each dire surmise—away!
My gracious God would not display
His glories to inflame my heart,
If I were destined to depart.
He would not cruelly deride
My soul with bliss to be denied;
Nor kindle love to pant in vain,
And rack me with augmented pain.
No, His own self will satisfy
The wishes He has raised so high.

Davies, Samuel. *Collected Poems of Samuel Davies.*
Gainsville: Scholars' Facsimiles & Reprints, 1968, pp. 117-118
("Devout Ejaculations and Soliloquies," Number 1).

Divine Breathings

AUGUSTUS TOPLADY

I groan from sin to be set free,
From self to be released;
Oh, take me, take me unto Thee,
My everlasting rest!

Come, O my Savior, come away,
Into my soul descend;
No longer from Thy creature stay,
My author, and my end!

The bliss Thou hast for me prepared,
No longer be delayed;
Come, my exceeding great reward,
For whom I first was made.

Thou all our works in us hast wrought,
Our good is all divine;
The praise of every virtuous thought,
And righteous work is Thine.

'Tis not of him that wills or runs,
That labors or desires;
In answer to my Savior's groans,
Thy love my breast inspires.

The meritorious cause I see,
That precious blood divine;
And I, since Jesus died for me,
Shall live forever Thine.

Toplady, Augustus. *The Works of Augustus Toplady,*
London: J. Chidley, 1837, p. 910.

Retirement

JOHN NEWTON

Far from the world, O Lord, I flee,
From strife and tumult far;
From scenes where Satan wages still
His most successful war.

The calm retreat, the silent shade,
With prayer and praise agree,
And seem by Thy sweet bounty made,
For those who follow Thee.

There if Thy Spirit touch the soul,
And grace her mean abode,
Oh, with what peace, and joy, and love,
She communes with her God.

There, like the nightingale, she pours
Her solitary lays,
Nor asks a witness of her song,
Nor thirsts for human praise.

Author and Guardian of my life,
Sweet Source of light divine,
And all harmonious names in one,
My Savior, Thou art mine.

What thanks I owe Thee, and what love,
A boundless, endless store,
Shall echo through the realms above,
When time shall be no more.

Newton, John. *The Works of the Rev. John Newton.*
Edinburgh: Thomas Nelson, 1841, p. 619.

The Ever-Faithful Instructor

LAW OF GOD

The law sends us to the gospel for our justification;
the gospel sends us to the law to frame our way of life.

— SAMUEL BOLTON

The Ever-Faithful Instructor
LAW OF GOD

The function of God's holy moral law is to show us what is good and acceptable, and what is sinful and displeasing to God. The law will send desperate sinners to the gospel for right standing with God, for who could possibly keep the requirements of such a high standard? The law shows us our need for Christ, the second Adam, who perfectly obeyed in every motive and action this holy law. His perfect obedience has been imputed to the account of the children God has given Him.

Furthermore, as forgiven, adopted children of the Most High Holy One, the law instructs us how to live a life that is pleasing to Him out of love and gratitude for the salvation He has bestowed. Ours is a free and evangelical obedience. We obey the law because we have been given a new heart, and this new heart now has a desire to obey the Savior. The Christian life is a reformation that rises out of a reformed motive, and that again out of a reformed heart.

A correct teaching of Scripture will enable us to understand that salvation is without our works (we are justified by Christ's cross work alone), though there is no salvation without works (for our obedience is a result of a regenerate heart—a new nature). Yes, our good works are necessary, for they give evidence of a new nature, but they are never meritorious. We merit eternal life and adoption into God's family by Christ's work alone.

The law is indeed a dependable instructor, for it shows us our need of the Savior, sending us to the cross for forgiveness and Christ's righteousness. Then from the foot of the cross we run back to this teacher to tell us how to live our lives from a motive of love and gratitude to our blessed Savior. May we pay close attention and show respect to our ever-faithful instructor.

Conviction of Sin by the Law

ISAAC WATTS

Lord, how secure my conscience was,
And felt no inward dread!
I was alive without the law,
And thought my sins were dead.

My hopes of heav'n were firm and bright;
But since the precept came,
With a convincing pow'r and light,
I find how vile I am.

My guilt appeared but small before,
Till terribly I saw
How perfect, holy, just, and pure,
Was Thine eternal law.

Then felt my soul the heavy load,
My sins revived again;
I had provoked a dreadful God,
And all my hopes were slain.

I'm like a helpless captive, sold
Under the pow'r of sin;
I cannot do the good I would,
Nor keep my conscience clean.

My God, I cry with every breath
For some kind pow'r to save,
To break the yoke of sin and death,
And thus redeem the slave.

Watts, Isaac. *The Psalms and Hymns of Isaac Watts.*
Morgan: Soli Deo Gloria Publications, 1997, pp. 374-375.

The Ten Commandments

RALPH ERSKINE

1. No God but Me thou shalt adore,
   I am thy God alone.

2. No image frame to bow before,
   But idols all dethrone.

3. God's glorious name take not in vain,
   For be revered He will.

4. His sacred Sabbath don't profane,
   Mind it is holy still.

5. To parents render due respect,
   This may thy life prolong.

6. All murder shun and malice check,
   To no man's life do wrong.

7. From thoughts of whoredom base abstain,
   From words and actions vile.

8. Shun theft and all unlawful gain,
   Nor gather wealth by guile.

9. False witness flee, and slandering spite,
   Nor wilful lies invent.

10. Don't covet what's thy neighbor's right,
    Nor harbor discontent.

Erskine, Ralph. *Erskine's Sermons and Practical Works.* Aberdeen: A. King & Co., 1863, VII:416-417.

The Burdened Sinner

JOHN NEWTON

Ah, what can I do,
Or where be secure?
If justice pursue,
What heart can endure?
The heart breaks asunder,
Though hard as a stone,
When God speaks in thunder,
And makes Himself known.

With terror I read
My sins heavy score;
The numbers exceed
The sands on the shore.
Guilt makes me unable
To stand or to flee;
So Cain murdered Abel,
And trembled like me.

Each sin, like his blood,
With a terrible cry,
Calls loudly on God,
To strike from on high;
Nor can my repentance,
Extorted by fear,
Reverse the just sentence,
'Tis just, though severe.

The case is too plain,
I have my own choice;
Again, and again,
I slighted His voice,
His warnings neglected,
His patience abused,
His gospel rejected,
His mercy refused.

And must I then go,
Forever to dwell
In torments and woe,
With devils in hell?
Oh, where is the Savior
I scorned in times past?
His Word in my favor
Would save me at last.

Lord Jesus on Thee
I venture to call,
Oh, look upon me,
The vilest of all.
For whom didst Thou languish,
And bleed on the tree?
Oh, pity my anguish,
And say, "'Twas for thee."

A case such as mine
Will honor Thy pow'r;
All hell will repine,
All heav'n will adore;
If in condemnation,
Strict justice takes place,
It shines in salvation,
More glorious through grace.

Newton, John. *The Works of the Rev. John Newton.*
Edinburgh: Thomas Nelson, 1841, p. 606.

Jehovah Tsidkenu
(The Lord Our Righteousness)
ROBERT MURRAY McCHEYNE

I once was a stranger to grace and to God,
I knew not my danger, and felt not my load;
Though friends spoke in rapture of Christ on the tree,
Jehovah Tsidkenu was nothing to me.

I oft read with pleasure, to soothe or engage,
Isaiah's wild measure and John's simple page;
But even when they pictured the blood-sprinkled tree,
Jehovah Tsidkenu seemed nothing to me.

Like tears from the daughters of Zion that roll,
I wept when the waters went over His soul;
Yet thought not that my sins had nailed to the tree,
Jehovah Tsidkenu—'twas nothing to me.

When free grace awoke me, by light from on high,
Then legal fears shook me, I trembled to die;
No refuge, no safety in self could I see,
Jehovah Tsidkenu my Savior must be.

My terrors all vanished before the sweet name;
My guilty fears banished, with boldness I came
To drink at the fountain, life-giving and free;
Jehovah Tsidkenu is all things to me.

Jehovah Tsidkenu, my treasure and boast!
Jehovah Tsidkenu, I ne'er can be lost!
In Thee I shall conquer by flood and by field,
My cable, my anchor, my breastplate and shield!

E'en treading the valley, the shadow of death,
This watchword shall rally my faltering breath;
For while from life's fever my God sets me free,
Jehovah Tsidkenu, my death song shall be.

McCheyne, Robert Murray. *The Life and Remains, Letters, Lectures, and Poems of the Rev. Robert Murray McCheyne,* Edited by Rev. Andrew A. Bonar, Robert Carter, NY, 1873, pp. 356-357.

Justification by Faith, Not by Works

ISAAC WATTS

Vain are the hopes the sons of men,
On their own works have built;
Their hearts by nature all unclean,
And all their actions guilt.

Let Jew and Gentile stop their mouths,
Without a murm'ring word,
And the whole race of Adam stand
Guilty before the Lord.

In vain we ask God's righteous law
To justify us now;
Since to convince and to condemn
Is all the law can do.

Jesus, how glorious is Thy grace!
When in Thy name we trust,
Our faith receives a righteousness
That makes the sinner just.

Watts, Isaac. *The Psalms and Hymns of Isaac Watts.*
Morgan: Soli Deo Gloria Publications, 1997, pp. 362-363

The Heart Healed and Changed by Mercy

JOHN NEWTON

Sin enslaved me many years,
And led me bound and blind;
Till at length a thousand fears
Came swarming o'er my mind.
Where, I said in deep distress,
Will these sinful pleasures end?
How shall I secure my peace,
And make the Lord my friend?

Friends and ministers said much
The gospel to enforce;
But my blindness still was such,
I chose a legal course.
Much I fasted, watched, and strove,
Scarce would show my face abroad;
Feared, almost, to speak or move,
A stranger still to God.

Thus, afraid to trust His grace,
Long time did I rebel;
Till, despairing of my case,
Down at His feet I fell.
Then my stubborn heart He broke,
And subdued me to His sway,
By a simple word he spoke,
"Thy sins are done away."

Newton, John. *The Works of the Rev. John Newton.*
Edinburgh: Thomas Nelson, 1841, p. 624.

Law and Gospel

SAMUEL DAVIES

With conscious fear and humble awe,
I view the terrors of the law;
Condemned at that tremendous bar,
I shrink, I tremble, and despair.

But hark, salvation in my ears,
Sounds sweetly and dispels my fears;
Jesus appears, and by His cross,
Fulfills His Father's broken laws.

Jesus, Saviour! dearest name!
By Him alone salvation came;
Terror, destruction and despair,
Where e'er I look besides, appear.

Adam, my head and father fell,
And sunk his offspring down to hell;
And the dread sword of justice waits,
To guard me from the heavenly gates.

Unnumbered crimes of dreadful names
Call loud for everlasting flames;
And all the duties I have done,
Can neither merit, nor atone.

Yet weak and guilty as I am,
I fix my trust on Jesus' name.
Jesus, whose righteousness alone
Can for the deepest crimes atone.

On Him, my soul, on Him rely;
The terms are fixed—Believe, or die.
Thee let the glorious gospel draw,
Or perish by the fiery law.

Davies, Samuel. *Collected Poems of Samuel Davies.*
Gainsville: Scholars' Facsimiles & Reprints, 1968, pp.93-94.

The Law and Gospel Distinguished

ISAAC WATTS

The law commands, and makes us know
What duties to our God we owe;
But 'tis the gospel must reveal
Where lies our strength to do His will.

The law discovers guilt and sin,
And shows how vile our hearts have been;
Only the gospel can express
Forgiving love and cleansing grace.

What curses does the law denounce
Against the man that fails but once!
But in the gospel Christ appears,
Pard'ning the guilt of num'rous years.

My soul, no more attempt to draw
Thy life and comfort from the law;
Fly to the hope the gospel gives;
The man that trusts the promise lives.

Watts, Isaac. *The Psalms and Hymns of Isaac Watts.*
Morgan: Soli Deo Gloria Publications, 1997, pp. 488-489.

The Difference between the Law and the Gospel

RALPH ERSKINE

The law supposing I have all,
Does ever for perfection call.
The gospel suits my total want,
And all the law can seek does grant.

The law could promise life to me,
If my obedience perfect be;
But grace does promise life upon
My Lord's obedience alone.

The law says, "Do, and life you'll win";
But grace says, "Live, for all is done."
The former cannot ease my grief;
The latter yields me full relief.

By law convinced of sinful breach;
By gospel grace I comfort reach.
The one my condemnation bears;
The other justifies and clears.

The law shows my arrears are great;
The gospel freely pays my debt.
The first does me the bankrupt curse;
The last does bless and fill my purse.

The law will not abate a mite;
The gospel all the sum will quite.
There God in threatenings is arrayed,
But here in promises displayed.

The law and gospel disagree,
Like Hagar, Sarah, bond and free.
The former's Hagar's servitude;
The latter's Sarah's happy brood.

To Sinai black, and Zion fair,
The Word does law and grace compare.
Their cursing and their blessing vie
With Ebal and Gerizzam high.

The law excludes not boasting vain,
But rather feeds it to my bane;
But gospel grace allows no boasts,
Save in the King, the Lord of hosts.

The law still irritates my sin,
And hardens my proud heart therein;
But grace's melting power renews,
And my corruption strong subdues.

The law with thunder, Sinai-like,
Does always dread and terror speak;
The gospel makes a joyful noise,
And charms me with a still, calm voice.

The legal trumpet war proclaims,
In wrathful threats, and fire, and flames;
The gospel pipe, a peaceful sound,
Which spreads a kindly breath around.

The law is weak through sinful flesh;
The gospel brings recruits afresh.
The first a killing letter wears;
The last a quickening spirit bears.

The law that seeks perfection's height,
Yet gives no strength, nor offers might;
But precious gospel tidings glad,
Declare where all is to be had.

From me alone the law does crave,
What grace affirms in Christ I have;
When therefore law pursuits enthrall,
I send the law to grace for all.

The law brings terror to molest;
The gospel gives the weary rest.
The one does flags of death display;
The other shows the living way.

The law by Moses was expressed;
The glorious gospel came by Christ.
The first dim nature's light may trace;
The last is only known by grace.

The law may rouse me from my sloth,
To faith and to repentance both;
And though the law commandeth each,
Yet neither of them can it teach.

Nor will accept for current coin
The duties which it does enjoin;
It seeks all, but accepts no less
Than constant, perfect righteousness.

The gospel, on the other hand,
Although it issue no command,
But strictly viewed, does whole consist
In promises and offers blessed.

Yet does it many duties teach,
Which legal light could never reach;
Thus faith, repentance, and the like,
Are fire that gospel engines strike.

They have acceptance here through grace,
The law affords them no such place;
Yet still they come through both their hands,
Through gospel teachings, law commands.

The law's a house of bondage sore;
The gospel opens the prison door.
The first me hampered in its net;
The law at freedom kindly set.

The precept craves, the gospel gives;
While that me presses, this relieves;
And or affords the strength I lack,
Or takes the burden off my back.

The law requires on pain of death;
The gospel courts with loving breath.
While that conveys a deadly wound;
This makes me perfect, whole and sound.

Their viewing how diseased I am,
I here perceive the healing balm;
Afflicted there with sense of need,
But here refreshed with meet remede.

The law's a charge for what I owe;
The gospel my discharge to show.
The one a scene of fears doth ope;
The other is the door of hope.

An angry God the law revealed;
The gospel shows Him reconciled.
By that I know He was displeased;
By this I see His wrath appeased.

The law thus shows the divine ire,
And nothing but consuming fire.
The gospel brings the olive branch,
And blood the burning fire to quench.

The law still shows a fiery face;
The gospel shows a throne of grace.
There justice rides alone in state;
But here she takes the mercy-seat.

Lo, in the law Jehovah dwells,
But Jesus is concealed;
Whereas the gospel's nothing else
But Jesus Christ revealed.

Erskine, Ralph. *Erskine's Sermons and Practical Works.*
Aberdeen: A. King & Co., 1863, VII:270-272.

The Harmony between the Law and the Gospel

RALPH ERSKINE

The law's a tutor much in vogue,
To gospel grace a pedagogue;
The gospel to the law no less
Than its full end for righteousness.

When once the fiery law of God
Has chased me to the gospel road;
Then back unto the law
Most kindly gospel grace will draw.

When by the law to grace I'm schooled;
Grace by the law will have me ruled;
Hence, if I don't the law obey,
I cannot keep the gospel way.

When I the gospel news believe,
Obedience to the law I give;
And that both in its federal dress,
And as a rule of holiness.

Lo, in my head I render all
For which the fiery law can call;
His blood unto its fire was fuel,
His Spirit shapes me to its rule.

When law and gospel kindly meet,
To serve each other both unite;
Sweet promises, and stern commands,
Do work to one another's hands.

The divine law demands no less
Than human perfect righteousness;
The gospel gives it this and more,
E'en divine righteousness in store,

Whate'er the righteous law require,
The gospel grants its whole desire.
Are law commands exceeding broad?
So is the righteousness of God.

How great so'er the legal charge,
The gospel payment's equal large;
No less by man the law can bray,
When grace provides a God to pay.

The law makes gospel banquets sweet;
The gospel makes the law complete.
Lawsuits to grace's storehouse draw;
Grace decks and magnifies the law.

Both law and gospel close combine,
To make each other's lustre shine;
The gospel all lawbreakers shames;
The law all gospel-slighters damns.

The law is holy, just, and good;
All this the gospel seals with blood,
And clears the royal law's just dues,
With dearly purchased revenues.

The law commands me to believe;
The gospel saving faith does give.
The law enjoins me to repent;
The gospel gives my tears a vent.

What in the gospel mint is coined,
The same is in the law enjoined:
Whatever gospel tidings teach,
The law's authority doth reach.

Here join the law and gospel hands,
What this me teaches, that commands;
What virtuous forms the gospel please,
The same the law doth authorize.

And thus the law commandment seals
Whatever gospel grace reveals;
The gospel also for my good
Seals all the law demands with blood.

The law most perfect still remains,
And every duty full contains;
The gospel its perfection speaks,
And therefore gives whate'er it seeks.

Next, what by law I'm bound unto,
The same the gospel makes me do;
What perceptively that can crave,
This effectively can engrave.

All that by precepts heaven expects,
Free grace by promises effects;
To what the law by fear may move,
To that the gospel leads by love.

To run to work, the law commands;
The gospel gives me feet and hands.
The one requires that I obey;
The other does the power convey.

What in the law has duty's place,
The gospel changes to a grace;
Hence legal duties therein named,
Are herein gospel graces famed.

The precepts check me when I stray;
The promise holds me in the way.
That shows my folly when I roam;
And this most kindly brings me home.

Law threats and precepts both, I see,
With gospel promises agree;
They to the gospel are a fence,
And it to them a maintenance.

The law will justify all those
Who with the gospel ransom close;
The gospel too approves for aye
All those that do the law obey.

The righteous law condemns each man
That dare reject the gospel plan;
The holy gospel none will save,
On whom it won't the law engrave.

When Christ the tree of life did climb,
I see both law and grace in Him;
In Him the law its end does gain;
In Him the promise is *Amen.*

The law makes grace's pasture sweet,
Grace makes the law my savory meat;
Yea, sweeter than the honeycomb,
When grace and mercy brings it home.

The precepts of the law me sow,
What fruits of gratitude I owe;
But gospel grace begets the brood,
And moves me to the gratitude.

Law terrors panse the putrid sore,
And gospel grace applies the cure;
The one ploughs up the fallow ground;
The other sows the seed around.

A rigid master was the law,
Demanding brick, denying straw;
But when the gospel tongue it sings,
It bids me fly, and gives me wings.

Both law and gospel close unite,
Are seen with more solace,
When truth and mercy kindly meet,
In fair Emmanuel's face.

Erskine, Ralph. *Erskine's Sermons and Practical Works.*
Aberdeen: A. King & Co., 1863, VII:273-275.

The Most Joyful News

GOSPEL OF CHRIST

Now then, we are ambassadors for Christ,
As though God were pleading through us:
We implore you on Christ's behalf,
Be reconciled to God.
For He made Him who knew no sin to be sin for us,
That we might become the righteousness of God in Him.

— 2 CORINTHIANS 5:20-21

The Most Joyful News
GOSPEL OF CHRIST

"If a herald were sent to a besieged city with the tidings that no terms of capitulation would be offered, but that every rebel without exception should be put to death, I think he would go with lingering footsteps, halting by the way to let out his heavy heart in sobs and groans; but if instead he were commissioned to go to the gates with the white flag to proclaim a free pardon, a general act of amnesty, surely he would run as though he had wings to his heels, with a joyful eagerness, to tell to his fellow-citizens the good pleasure of their merciful king. Heralds of salvation, ye carry the most joyful of all messages to the sons of men!" (Spurgeon, Charles. *Spurgeon's Sermons*, Vol 9. Grand Rapids: Baker Book House, 1883, p. 245.)

As heralds to a besieged city, what is our message? Think of the last conversation you had with your unsaved neighbor, coworker, relative, or friend. Did you bring up the topic of their eternal destiny? Did you talk about their need as sinners of Jesus Christ? Or did you talk about sports, politics, stock options, movies, or the nightly newscast? While these may be nice topics for casual chats, have any of your conversations ever gotten beyond them? Or perhaps your thoughts were "I shouldn't worry about their captivity right now. I'm sure there will be an opportunity tomorrow to take care of it." Why are we so reluctant to speak of the best news of all—Jesus Christ and the gospel?

All mankind is held captive by the guilt of their sin, by the pain of living in a fallen world, and by the sure prospect of death. These documents were delivered at the fall in the Garden of Eden. Christians have been commissioned by the merciful King to bring a second dispatch, the most joyful of all communications: "There is a free pardon for all who will come to Christ confessing they are sinners in need of a Savior!" Is there better news than that?

The Glorious Gospel of the Blessed God

SAMUEL STENNETT

What wisdom, majesty, and grace,
Through all the gospel shine!
'Tis God that speaks, and we confess
The doctrine most divine.

Down from His starry throne on high,
The almighty Savior comes;
Lays His bright robes of glory by,
And feeble flesh assumes.

The mighty debt that sinners owed,
Upon the cross He pays;
Then through the clouds ascends to God,
'Mid shouts of loftiest praise.

There He, our great High Priest, appears
Before His Father's throne;
Mingles His merits with our tears,
And pours salvation down.

Great God, with reverence we adore
Thy justice and Thy grace;
And on Thy faithfulness and pow'r
Our firm dependence place.

Stennett, Samuel. *The Works of Samuel Stennett, D.D.*
London: Thomas Tegg. 1824, p. 534.

Salvation Recovered for Man by Jesus Christ

AUGUSTUS TOPLADY

Zion, awake, put on thy strength,
Resume thy beautiful array;
The promised Savior comes at length,
To chase thy guilt and grief away;
Thee for His purchase God shall own,
And save thee by His dying Son.

Jerusalem, be holy now,
Satan no more shall dwell in thee;
Washed from thy sin, and white as snow,
Prepare thy God-made-man to see;
Prepare Immanuel to behold,
And hear His peaceful message told.

Shake off the dust, arise with speed;
Too long hast thou a captive been.
Redemption's near, lift up thine head,
And cast away the chains of sin;
Forth from thy prison come, and shake
The yoke of bondage from thy neck.

Though ye have sold yourselves for nought,
And forfeited your claim to heaven,
Accept the Savior's love unbought;
Your treason now is all forgiven;
My blood the fallen race restores,
And saves without desert of yours.

Ye desert places, sing for joy;
Lost man, your hymns of wonder raise;
Let holy shouts invade the sky,
And ev'ry altar flame with praise;
For I, almighty to redeem,
Have comforted Jerusalem.

My arm's made bare for your defense,
To save My Church from Satan's power,
Depart, depart, come out from thence,
Defile yourselves with sin no more;
Be pure, ye priests, who preach My Word,
And bear the vessels of the Lord.

Look out and see Immanuel come,
Myriads to sprinkle with His blood;
He many nations shall bring home,
And save them from the wrath of God;
And earth's remotest bounds shall see
The great salvation wrought by Me.

Toplady, Augustus. *The Works of Augustus Toplady.*
London: J. Chidley, 1837, p. 901.

The Word Was God

MATTHEW HALE

The Word was God, and yet made flesh, a strange
Mysterious change, and yet without change;
Two natures, God and man, most strictly joined
Into one Person, yet distinct remained.

But why this great conjunction? Or what end
Could countervail it? What did it portend
Of equal moment? Or what great event
Required such means for its accomplishment?

Was it to save poor fallen man? Alas,
A worm, a sinful worm; one that still was
A rebel to his Maker. How could he
For love or pity hope? Much less to be

Redeemed at such a rate? But, if he should
Hope for a pardon, yet his Sovereign could,
On easier terms, life and a pardon give;
His only word could bid and make him live.

Peace, busy thoughts, this depth is too profound
For you to fathom! Angels cannot sound
This ocean; but yet, if needs you will
Be roving after it, and searching still,

Let this compose you—God's design herein,
Next to His own dear glory, was to bring
Man to enjoy his Maker, the chief good,
Wherein alone his blessed condition stood,

Which once he had, and lost; and since no way
We have our God again to re-enjoy,
But Him to know and love; each circumstance
In this design are fitted to advance

Those two important means; and yet because
The wise Creator seldom breaks these laws
Himself hath set, He chooseth to improve
And to advance that knowledge and that love

In this great work, by means of such a rate
As might be powerful, yet accommodate
And proper to our nature; such as take
And suit best with His creatures' frame and make.

Should God in His bright majesty appear
To teach us Him to know, we could not bear
The brightness of His glory; that pure light
Would dissipate our nature, or affright,

Instead of teaching us. Again, should we
Learn only from a mortal man, 'twould be
Too weak and impotent. God therefore chose
A middle way, namely, to interpose

A veil of flesh before that majesty,
Which if a mortal should but see, he'd die.
This veil the glorious Son of God doth take,
And under it with men converse He makes,

Shows them His Father's will. And none so if
To teach us what to know of God, for it
Lay best within His knowledge. This He speaks
Not in the voice of thunder, neither breaks

Into seraphic raptures, but complies
With human methods; clothes great mysteries
In plain discourses; useth arguments
That are most forcible to gain assent

From human reason; gently stoops to sense
In miracles, the greatest evidence
Of truth our nature knows, and in this still
And gentle voice, His hearers' souls He fills

With profitable truths; yet to evince
That God was in that voice, and evidence
His mission and His doctrine both divine,
He lets so much of native glory shine,

Refracted through this cloud of flesh, such light
As sweetly might convince, but not affright.
And since our Maker knows nothing incites
Our love with greater fervor, nor invites

Our human nature more, than when we see
Surpassing undeserved love to be
First shown to us, He chooseth to express
His love so highly to us, and to dress

The whole economy of man's redemption
With so much tenderness, such condescension,
Such matchless instances that did excel
Example, never had a parallel.

Poor wretched man, thou was a lost, undone,
Distressed, worthless, fallen creature, one
That hadst rebelled against thy God, and though
Under the chains of death thou didst not know,

Nor feel thy bondage, that didst rather scorn
Then seek a pardon; yet, in this forlorn
Estate of then, thy injured Maker sends
His Son to seek and save thee. He descends

To save His rebel; though He did not need.
He seeks thy love, becomes a man to bleed
And die for thee, an enemy that never
So much as asked help, and to deliver

Thy soul from endless death, and with His own
Abasement to procure for thee a crown.
And tell me now, if ever any thing
Could be contrived by less than heaven to bring

Man to return and love his God, that fits
So well our frame, or that so kindly hits
Our best affections' strings. Sure none but He,
Who knew, because He made our hearts, could see

What might endear it most, exactly knew
All the approaches, every avenue
That gives access to it, could only frame
A means so suitable to win the same.

Methinks in this design I cannot tell
Whether the wisdom or the love excel;
Both wonderful, and both may justly move
And raise our admiration and our love.

And he that thinks but of it, and yet can
Deny his dear-bought love, hath put off Man.

Hale, Matthew. *Contemplations, Moral and Divine.*
London: Sherwood, Neely, & Jones, n.d. II:597-600.

A Song of Praise for Deliverance

JOHN MASON

I that am drawn out of the depth,
Will sing upon the shore;
I that in hell's dark suburbs lay,
Pure mercy will adore.
The terrors of the living God
My soul did so affright,
I feared lest I should be condemned
To an eternal night.

Kind was the pity of my friends,
But could not ease my smart;
Their words, indeed, did reach my case,
But could not reach my heart.
Ah, then, what was this world to me,
To whom God's Word was dark;
Who in my dungeon could not see
One beam or shining spark?

What, then, were all the creatures' smiles,
When the Creator frowned?
My days were nights, my life was death,
My being was my wound.
Tortured and racked with hellish fears,
When God the blow should give;
Mine eyes did fail, my heart did sink;
Then mercy bid me live.

God's furnace doth in Zion stand,
But Zion's God sits by;
As the refiner views his gold
With an observant eye.
God's thoughts are high, His love is wise,
His wounds a cure intend;
And though He doth not always smile,
He loves unto the end.

Thy love is constant to its line,
Though clouds oft come between;
Oh, could my faith but pierce these clouds,
It might be always seen.
But I am weak, and forced to cry,
Take up my soul to Thee;
Then, as Thou ever art the same,
So shall I ever be.

Then shall I ever, ever sing,
While Thou dost ever shine;
I have Thine own dear pledge for this,
Lord, Thou art ever mine.

Mason, John. *Spiritual Songs, or Songs of Praise to Almighty God.*
Edinburgh: James Taylor, 1880, pp. 84-86.

Thy Golden Chain of Grace

EDWARD TAYLOR

A state, a state, oh, dungeon state indeed!
In which me headlong, long ago sin pitched;
As dark as pitch; where nastiness doth breed;
And filth defiles, and I am with it ditched.
A sinful state; this pit no water's in it.
A bugbare state, as black as any ink.

I once a singing on the summit high
Among the celestial choir in music sweet;
On highest bough of paradisal joy;
Glory and innocence did in me meet.
I as a goldfinch nightingale, tuned o'er
Melodious songs before glory's palace door.

But on this bough I tuning perched not long;
The infernal foe shot out a shaft from hell;
A fiery dart piled with sins poison strong;
That struck my heart, and down I headlong fell.
And from the highest pinnacle of light
Into this lowest pit more dark than night.

A pit indeed of sin; no water's here;
Whose bottom's furthest off from heaven bright.
And is next door to hell gate; to it near;
And here I dwell in sad and solemn night.
My goldfinch angel feathers dappled in
Hell's scarlet dye fat, blood-red grown with sin.

I in this pit all destitute of light
Crammed full of horrid darkness, here do crawl
Up over head, and ears, in nauseous plight;
And swinelike wallow in this mire and gall.
No heavenly dews nor holy waters drill;
Nor sweet air breeze, nor comfort here distill.

Here for companions, are fears, heartaches, grief,
Frogs, toads, newts, bats, horrid hobgoblins, ghosts,
Ill spirits haunt this pit; and no relief;
Nor cord can fetch me hence in creature's coasts.
I who once lodged at heavens palace gate,
With full fledged angels, now possess this fate.

But yet, my Lord, Thy golden chain of grace,
Thou canst let down, and draw me up into
Thy holy air, and glory's happy place,
Out from these hellish damps and pit so low.
And if thy grace shall do it, my harp I'll raise,
Whose strings touched by this grace, will twang Thy praise.

Taylor, Edward. *The Poetical Works of Edward Taylor.*
Princeton: Princeton University Press, 1943, pp. 172-173,
Meditation Seventy-Seven, Second Series.

The Blessedness of Gospel Times

ISAAC WATTS

How beautiful are their feet,
Who stand on Zion's hill;
Who bring salvation on their tongues,
And words of peace reveal!

How charming is their voice;
How sweet the tidings are!
"Zion, behold thy Savior King;
He reigns and triumphs here."

How happy are our ears,
That hear this joyful sound,
Which kings and prophets waited for,
And sought, but never found!

How blessed are our eyes,
That see this heavenly light!
Prophets and kings desired it long,
But died without the sight.

The watchmen join their voice,
And tuneful notes employ;
Jerusalem breaks forth in songs,
And deserts learn the joy.

The Lord makes bare His arm,
Through all the earth abroad;
Let every nation now behold
Their Savior and their God!

Watts, Isaac. *The Psalms and Hymns of Isaac Watts.*
Morgan: Soli Deo Gloria Publications, 1997, p. 298.

God Saying to the Soul, That He Is Its Salvation

PHILIP DODDRIDGE

Salvation, oh, melodious sound,
To wretched dying men;
Salvation, that from God proceeds,
And leads to God again.

Rescued from hell's eternal gloom,
From fiends, and fires, and chains;
Raised to a paradise of bliss,
Where love and glory reigns.

But, oh, may a degenerate soul,
Sinful and weak as mine,
Presume to raise a trembling eye
To blessings so divine?

The luster of so bright a bliss
My feeble heart o'er bears;
And unbelief almost perverts
The promise into tears.

My Savior God, no voice but Thine,
These dying hopes can raise;
Speak Thy salvation to my soul,
And turn its tears to praise.

My Savior God, this broken voice,
Transported shall proclaim;
And call on the angelic harps,
To sound so sweet a name.

Doddridge, Philip. *The Miscellaneous Works of Philip Doddridge.*
London: Joseph Ogle Robinson, 1830, p. 990.

Cords of Love

RALPH ERSKINE

Seek God while yet He may be found,
Call on Him while He's near;
While grace's trump, the joyful sound
Of mercy strikes your ear.

Oh, let the wicked change his way,
And the unrighteous man,
His thoughts, and legal hopes, that stray,
Cross to the gospel plan.

And let him now return to God,
The Lord our righteousness;
Who, through the merit of His blood,
In mercy will him bless.

To our God let him run betimes,
For gracious will He be;
And for his multitude of crimes
Will pardons multiply.

Let, saith the Lord, My boundless grace
Move guilty souls to come,
And trust Me with their desp'rate case
When hopeless thoughts do roam.

Because My thoughts and ways divine
Are not as yours; for why?
All yours are base and low, but Mine
Immensely great and high.

For as the heav'ns, in height and space,
Transcend your earthly boors;
Much more My thoughts and ways of grace
Surmount all thoughts of yours.

Great God, then bid the mountains move;
Our sins that reach the sky,
Be melted down with flames of love,
More infinitely high.

Erskine, Ralph. *Erskine's Sermons and Practical Works.*
Aberdeen: A. King & Co., 1863, VII:559-560
("God's Drawing Them to Himself with Cords of Love").

Refining Fuller

AUGUSTUS TOPLADY

Refining Fuller, make me clean,
On me Thy costly pearl bestow;
Thou art Thyself the pearl I prize,
The only joy I seek below.

Disperse the clouds that damp my soul,
And make my heart unfit for Thee;
Cast me not off, but seal me now,
Thine own peculiar property.

Look on the wounds of Christ for me,
My sentence graciously reprieve;
Extend Thy peaceful scepter, Lord,
And bid the dying traitor live.

Though I transgressed the rules prescribed,
And dared the justice I adore;
Yet let Thy smiling mercy say,
"Depart in peace, and sin no more."

Toplady, Augustus. *The Works of Augustus Toplady.*
London: J. Chidley, 1837, p. 886 (Poem 1).

Expostulation

JOHN NEWTON

No words can declare,
No fancy can paint,
What rage and despair,
What hopeless complaint,
Fill Satan's dark dwelling,
The prison beneath,
What weeping, and yelling,
And gnashing of teeth!

Yet sinners will choose
This dreadful abode;
Each madly pursues
The dangerous road.
Though God give them warning,
They onward will go,
They answer with scorning,
And rush upon woe.

How sad to behold
The rich and the poor,
The young and the old,
All blindly secure!
All posting to ruin,
Refusing to stop;
Ah, think what you're doing,
While yet there is hope.

How weak is your hand,
To fight with the Lord!
How can you withstand
The edge of His sword?
What hope of escaping
For those who oppose,
When hell is wide gaping
To swallow His foes!

How oft have you dared
The Lord to His face!
Yet still you are spared
To hear of His grace;
Oh, pray for repentance
And life-giving faith,
Before the just sentence
Consign you to death.

It is not too late,
To Jesus to flee;
His mercy is great,
His pardon is free;
His blood has such virtue
For all that believe,
That nothing can hurt you,
If Him you receive.

Newton, John. *The Works of the Rev. John Newton.*
Edinburgh: Thomas Nelson, 1841, p. 604.

We Are Ambassadors for Christ

JOHN NEWTON

Thy message by the preacher seal,
And let Thy power be known,
That every sinner here may feel
The word is not his own.

Among the foremost of the throng,
Who dare Thee to Thy face,
He in rebellion stood too long,
And fought against Thy grace.

But grace prevailed, he mercy found,
And now by Thee is sent,
To tell his fellow rebels round,
And call them to repent.

In Jesus, God is reconciled,
The worst may be forgiven;
Come and He'll own you as a child,
And make you heirs of heaven.

Oh, may the Word of gospel truth
Your chief desires engage!
And Jesus be your Guide in youth,
Your joy in hoary age.

Perhaps the year that's now begun
May prove to some their last;
The sands of life may soon be run,
The day of grace be past.

Think, if you slight this embassy,
And will not warning take
When Jesus in the clouds you see,
What answer will you make?

Newton, John. *The Works of the Rev. John Newton.*
Edinburgh: Thomas Nelson, 1841, p. 580.

Travailing in Birth for Souls

JOHN NEWTON

What contradictions meet
In ministers employ!
It is a bitter sweet,
A sorrow full of joy;
No other post affords a place,
For equal honor or disgrace!

Who can describe the pain
Which faithful preachers feel,
Constrained to speak in vain,
To hearts as hard as steel?
Or who can tell the pleasures felt,
When stubborn hearts begin to melt?

The Savior's dying love,
The soul's amazing worth,
Their utmost efforts move,
And draw their bowels forth;
They pray, and strive, their rest departs,
Till Christ be formed in sinners' hearts.

If some small hope appear,
They still are not content;
But, with a jealous fear,
They watch for the event.
Too oft they find their hopes deceived,
Then how their inmost souls are grieved!

But when their pains succeed,
And from the tender blade,
The ripening ears proceed,
Their toils are overpaid.
No harvest-joy can equal theirs,
To find the fruit of all their cares.

On what has now been sown,
Thy blessing, Lord, bestow;
The power is Thine alone,
To make it spring and grow.
Do Thou the gracious harvest raise,
And Thou alone shalt have the praise.

Newton, John. *The Works of the Rev. John Newton.*
Edinburgh: Thomas Nelson, 1841, p. 580.

Buy Without Money

FREE GRACE

Ho! Everyone who thirsts, come to the waters;
And you who have no money, come, buy and eat.
Yes, come, buy wine and milk without money and without price.
Why do you spend money for what is not bread,
And your wages for what does not satisfy?
Listen carefully to Me, and eat what is good,
And let your soul delight itself in abundance.

— Isaiah 55:1-2

Buy Without Money
FREE GRACE

In this world we witness an assorted lot of consumers, trading and dealing in various commodities. But the one commodity needful for this world and the next is often passed by. Every now and then a weary, unsatisfied shopper catches a glimpse of "the pearl of great price." One look—one longing look—and the crazed consumerism has ended.

How may an enlightened soul have Christ and His benefits? How shall he be able to buy wares in His fair market? Checking his funds he finds none—an empty purse. But to his surprise it is in this empty purse he finds the invitation for a shopping spree in this market. Yes, extreme necessity and want, realizing one's spiritual poverty and even the monumental debt owed, oh, how the doors fly open to such a beggar!

Who shall foot the bill for the debt incurred by an empty handed sinner? It is Christ. He has said, "I will purchase this man's garments, these robes of righteousness, and all the blessed goods this man needs. I will cancel the debt owed and pay the bill for this thief of My Father's goods. Charge it to My account!"

The Poor Man's Market

SAMUEL RUTHERFORD

Our Lord's love is not so cruel as to let a poor man see Christ
    and heaven,
And never give him more, for want of money to buy.
Nay, I rather think Christ to be such fair market wares,
As buyers may have without money and without price.
And thus I know that it shall not stand upon my want of money;
For Christ upon His own charges must buy my wedding-garment,
And redeem the inheritance which I have forfeited,
And give His word for one the like of me,
Who am not law abiding of myself.
Poor folk must either borrow or beg from the rich;
And the only thing that commendeth sinners to Christ
Is extreme necessity and want.
Christ's love is ready to make and provide a ransom,
And money for a poor body who hath lost his purse.
"Ho, ye that have no money, come and buy"—
That is the poor man's market.

Rutherford, Samuel. *Letters of Samuel Rutherford.*
Edinburgh; Carlisle: Banner of Truth, 1984, p. 532.

The Free Gospel

RALPH ERSKINE

Ho, every thirsty soul, and all
That poor and needy are;
Here's water of salvation well
For you to come and share.

Here's freedom both from sin and woe,
And blessings all divine;
Here streams of love and mercy flow,
Like floods of milk and wine.

Approach the fountainhead of bliss,
That's open like the sea,
To buyers that are moneyless,
The poorest beggars free.

Why spend you all your wealth and pains,
For that which is not bread,
And for unsatisfying gains,
On which no soul can feed?

While vain ye seek, with earthly toys,
To fill an empty mind,
You lose immortal solid joys,
And feed upon the wind.

Incline your ear, and come to Me;
Hear, and your soul shall live;
For mercies sure, as well as free,
I bind Myself to give.

Erskine, Ralph. *Erskine's Sermons and Practical Works.*
Aberdeen: A. King & Co., 1863, VII:558-559.

The Fountain
(The Invitations of the Gospel)
SAMUEL DAVIES

Today the living streams of grace
Flow to refresh the thirsty soul;
Pardon and life and boundless bliss
In plenteous rivers round us roll.

Ho, ye that pine away and die,
Come, and your raging thirst allay;
Come all that will, here's rich supply,
A fountain that shall ne'er decay.

"Come all," the blessed Jesus cries,
"Freely My blessings I will give."
The spirit echoes back the voice,
And bids us freely drink and live.

The saints below, that do but taste,
And saints above, who drink at will,
Cry jointly, "Thirsty sinners! haste,
And drink, the spring's exhaustless still."

Let all that hear the joyful sound,
To spread it through the world unite;
From house to house proclaim it round,
Each man his fellow man invite.

Like thirsty flocks, come let us go;
Come every color, every age;
And while the living waters flow,
Let all their parching thirst assuage.

Davies, Samuel. *Collected Poems of Samuel Davies.*
Gainsville: Scholars' Facsimiles & Reprints, 1968, pp. 203-204.

The Sinner's Refuge

FRANCIS QUARLES

He that shall shed, with a presumptuous hand,
The blood of men, must by Thy just command
Be put to death; the murderer must die.
Thy law denies him refuge where to fly.

Great God, our hands have slain a Man; nay further,
They have committed a presumptuous murder
Upon a guiltless Man; nay, what is worse,
They have betrayed our Brother to the curse

Of a reproachful death; nay, what exceeds,
It is our Lord, our dying Savior bleeds;
Nay more, it is Thy Son, Thine only Son.
All this have we, all this our hands have done.

On what dear object shall we turn our eye?
Look to the law? Oh, by the law we die.
Is there no refuge, Lord? No place that shall
Secure our souls from death? Ah, none at all.

What shall poor mortals do? Thy laws are just,
And most irrevocable; shall we trust,
Or fly to our own merit, and be freed
By our own good works? If there were help indeed.

Is there no city for a soul to fly,
And save itself? Must we resolve to die?
Oh Infinite, oh—not to be expressed—
Nay, not to be conceived by the breast

Of men or angels, oh transcendent love,
Incomprehensible, as far above
The reach of man, as man's deserts are under
The sacred benefit of so blessed a wonder!

That very blood our sinful hands have shed
Cries loud for mercy, and those wounds do plead
For those that made them; He that pleads, forgives,
And is both God and Man—both dead and lives.

He whom we murdered is become our Guardian;
He's Man to suffer, and He's God to pardon.
Here's our protection; here's our Refuge City,
Whose living springs run piety and pity.

Go then, my soul, and pass the common bounds
Of passion; go and kneel before His wounds.
Thou need not fear; the very blood He spilled,
By grace, will plead thy pardon, not thy guilt.

Quarles, Francis. *The Complete Works in Prose and Verse of Francis Quarles.*
Lancashire: Blackburn, 1880, II:211-212.

Praise for Conversion

SAMUEL STENNETT

Come, ye that fear the Lord,
And listen, while I tell
How narrowly my feet escaped
The snares of death and hell.

The flattering joys of sense
Assailed my foolish heart,
While Satan with malicious skill
Guided the poisonous dart.

I fell beneath the stroke,
But fell to rise again;
My anguish roused me into life,
And pleasure sprung from pain.

Darkness and shame and grief,
Oppressed my gloomy mind;
I looked around me for relief,
But no relief could find,

At length to God I cried;
He heard my plaintive sigh;
He heard, and instantly He sent
Salvation from on high.

My drooping head He raised;
My bleeding wounds He healed;
Pardoned my sins, and, with a smile,
The gracious pardon sealed.

Oh, may I never forget
The mercy of my God;
Nor ever want a tongue to spread
His loudest praise abroad.

Stennett, Samuel. *The Works of Samuel Stennett, D.D.*
London: Thomas Tegg, 1824, pp. 548-549.

How Shall I Put Thee Among the Children

JOHN NEWTON

Alas, by nature how depraved,
How prone to every ill!
Our lives to Satan how enslaved,
How obstinate our will!

And can such sinners be restored,
Such rebels reconciled?
Can grace itself the means afford,
To make a foe a child?

Yes, grace has found the wondrous means,
Which shall effectual prove,
To cleanse us from our countless sins,
And teach our hearts to love.

Jesus for sinners undertakes,
And died that we may live;
His blood a full atonement makes,
And cries aloud, "Forgive."

Yet one thing more must grace provide,
To bring us home to God,
Or we shall slight the Lord who died,
And trample on His blood.

The Holy Spirit must reveal
The Savior's work and worth;
Then the hard heart begins to feel
A new and heavenly birth.

Thus bought with blood, and born again,
Redeemed and saved by grace,
Rebels in God's own house obtain
A son's and daughter's place.

Newton, John. *The Works of the Rev. John Newton.*
Edinburgh: Thomas Nelson, 184,. pp. 580-581.

Longing

GEORGE HERBERT

With sick and famished eyes,
With doubling knees and weary bones,
To Thee my cries,
To Thee my groans,
To Thee my sighs, my tears ascend—
No end?

My throat, my soul is hoary;
My heart is withered like a ground,
Which Thou dost curse.
My thoughts turn round,
And make me giddy. Lord, I fall,
Yet call.

From Thee all pity flows.
Mothers are kind, because Thou art,
And dost dispose
To them a part.
Their infants them, and they suck Thee
More free.

Bowels of pity, heart,
Lord of my soul, love of my mind,
Bow down Thine ear!
Let not the wind
Scatter my words, and in the same
Thy name!

Look on my sorrows round!
Mark well my furnace, oh what flames,
What heat abounds!
What griefs, what shames!
Consider Lord; Lord, bow Thine ear,
And hear!

Lord Jesus, Thou didst bow
Thy dying head upon the tree.
Oh, be not now
More dead to me,
Lord hear! Shall He that made the ear,
Not hear?

Behold, Thy dust doth stir;
It moves, it creeps, it aims at Thee:
Wilt Thou defer
To succor me,
Thy pile of dust, wherein each crumb
Says, "Come"?

To Thee help appertains.
Hast Thou left all things to their course,
And laid the reins
Upon the horse?
Is all locked? Hath a sinner's plea
No key?

Indeed the world's Thy book,
Where all things have their leaf assigned;
Yet a meek look
Hath interlined.
Thy board is full, yet humble guests
Find nests.

Thou tarriest, while I die,
And fall to nothing. Thou dost reign,
And rule on high,
While I remain
In bitter grief; yet I am stilled—
Thy child.

Lord, didst Thou leave Thy throne,
Not to relieve? How can it be,
That Thou art grown
Thus hard to me?
Were sin alive, good cause there were
To bear.

But now both sin is dead,
And all thy promises live and bid
That wants his head;
These speak and chide,
And in Thy bosom pour my tears,
As theirs.

Lord Jesus, heal my heart,
Which hath been broken now so long,
That every part
Hath got a tongue!
Thy beggars grow; rid them away
Today.

My love, my sweetness, hear!
By these Thy feet, at which my heart
Lies all the year,
Pluck out Thy dart,
And heal my troubled breast, which cries,
Which dies.

Herbert, George. *From Heaven or Hell upon Earth* by Nathanael Vincent.
London: Thomas Parkhurst, 1676.

Oh Lord, I Will Praise Thee

JOHN NEWTON

I will praise Thee every day,
Now Thine anger's turned away!
Comfortable thoughts arise
From the bleeding sacrifice.

Here, in the fair gospel-field,
Wells of free salvation yield
Streams of life a plenteous store,
And my soul shall thirst no more.

Jesus is become at length
My salvation and my strength;
And His praises shall prolong,
While I live, my pleasant song.

Praise ye, then, His glorious name,
Publish His exalted fame!
Still His worth your praise exceeds,
Excellent are all His deeds.

Raise again the joyful sound,
Let the nations roll it round!
Zion, shout, for this is He;
God, the Savior, dwells in thee.

Newton, John. *The Works of the Rev. John Newton.*
Edinburgh: Thomas Nelson, 1841, p. 544.

Room at the Gospel Feast

PHILIP DODDRIDGE

The King of heaven His table spreads,
And dainties crown the board;
Not paradise with all its joys
Could such delight afford.

Pardon and peace to dying men,
And endless life are given,
And the rich blood that Jesus shed
To raise the soul to heaven.

Ye hungry poor, that long have strayed
In sins' dark mazes, come.
Come from the hedges and highways,
And grace shall find you room.

Millions of souls, in glory now,
Were fed and feasted here;
And millions more, still on the way,
Around the board appear.

Yet is His house and heart so large,
That millions more may come;
Nor could the wide assembling world
Overfill the spacious room.

All things are ready; come away,
Nor weak excuses frame.
Crowd to your places at the feast,
And bless the Founder's name.

Doddridge, Philip. *The Miscellaneous Works of Philip Doddridge.*
London: Joseph Ogle Robinson, 1830, p. 1034.

Father to Thee in Christ I Fly

AUGUSTUS TOPLADY

Father, to Thee in Christ I fly,
What though my sins of crimson dye,
For Thy resentment call?
My crimes He did on Calv'ry bear,
The blood that flowed for sinners there
Shall cleanse me from them all.

Spirit divine, Thy power bring in;
Oh, raise me from this depth of sin,
Take off my guilty load;
Now let me live through Jesus' death,
And, being justified by faith,
May I have peace with God!

Foul as I am, deserving hell,
Thou cannot from Thy throne repel
A soul that leans on God;
My sins at Thy command shall be
Cast as a stone into the sea—
The sea of Jesus' blood.

Toplady, Augustus. *The Works of Augustus Toplady.*
London: J. Chidley, 1837, p. 889 (Poem XIII).

Prayer of King Manasseh

AUGUSTUS TOPLADY

Author of all in earth and sky,
From whom the stars derive their light,
When Thou art wroth the planets die,
And melt as nothing in Thy sight.

Measured by Thine almighty hand,
Unfathomed seas of liquid glass
Obedient, own Thy high command,
And keep the bounds they cannot pass.

Shut up by their restraining Lord,
They in their proper channels flow;
Obey Jehovah's sovereign word,
"Here, and no farther, shall ye go."

Thy terrors, as a blazing flame,
Devour and weigh the sinner down;
The mighty tremble at Thy name,
And nations quake beneath Thy frown.

Tremendous as Thy judgments are,
Thy pity too no limit knows;
Thine arm is stretched the meek to spare,
And terribly consume Thy foes.

With shame, great God, I own with me,
Thy waiting mercy long hath borne,
Yet would I not come back to Thee,
Proudly refusing to return.

When mercy called, I stopped my ear,
How did I from the Savior rove,
And, bent on death, refuse to hear
The voice of Thy inviting love!

Blind were my eyes, and hard my heart,
And proof against Thy striving grace;
I would from Thee, my Strength, depart,
And cease to walk in wisdom's ways.

But, lo, on Thee I fix my hope;
Be Thou my Friend and Advocate.
Gracious Redeemer, lift me up,
And raise me to my first estate.

Faith in Thy merit is Thy gift
By which Thou dost backsliders heal;
Impart it, gracious Lord, to lift
My abject soul from whence I fell.

Destruction shall not seize the just,
Whose sin already is forgiv'n,
Whom Thou hast rescued from the lost,
And numbered with the heirs of heav'n.

To sinners, of whom I am chief,
Thy healing promises pertain;
Who fell from Thee through unbelief,
By faith may be restored again.

Of boundless mercy I have need,
My sins have took deep hold of me;
In number they the grains exceed
That form the margin of the sea.

Meek on the earth Thy servant lies,
And humbly makes his sorrows known;
Unworthy to lift up my eyes
To heaven, my injured Maker's throne.

Bowed with my sense of sin, I faint,
Beneath the complicated load;
Father, attend my deep complaint,
I am Thy creature, Thou my God!

Though I have broke Thy righteous law,
Yet with me let Thy Spirit stay:
Thyself from me do not withdraw,
Not take my spark or hope away.

Mercy unlimited is Thine,
God of the Penitent Thou art;
The saving power of blood divine,
Shall wipe the anguish from my heart.

Then let not sin my ruin be,
Give me in Thee my rest to find:
Jesus, the sick have need of Thee,
The great Physician of mankind.

In my salvation, Lord, display
The triumphs of abounding grace;
Tell me my guilt is done away,
And turn my mourning into praise.

Reprieved so long from hell's abyss,
Thou will not hurl me there at last,
But cheer me with the smile of peace,
Nor look at my offences past.

Then shall I add my feeble song
To theirs who chant Thy praise on high,
And spread, with an immortal tongue,
Thy glory through the echoing sky.

Toplady, Augustus. *The Works of Augustus Toplady.*
London: J. Chidley, 1837, p. 899.

Applying for Relief to the All-Sufficiency of Christ

SAMUEL DAVIES

I hear the counsel of a Friend;
To the kind voice, my soul, attend.
"Come, sinners, wretched, blind, and poor,
Come, draw from My unbounded store."

"I only ask you to receive,
For freely I My blessings give."
Jesus, and are thy treasurers free,
Then I may dare to come to Thee?

I come for grace, that gold refined,
To enrich and beautify my mind,
Grace that will trials well endure,
By trials more divinely pure.

Naked I come for that bright dress,
Thy perfect spotless righteousness,
That glorious robe, so richly dyed
In Thine own blood, my shame to hide.

Like Bartimaeus, Lord, to Thee
I come; oh, give the blind to see!
E'en clay is eye-salve in Thine hand,
If Thou the blessing but command.

Poor, naked, blind I hither came,
Oh, let me not depart the same!
Let me return, all-gracious Lord,
Enriched, adorned, to sight restored.

Davies, Samuel. *Collected Poems of Samuel Davies.*
Gainsville: Scholars' Facsimiles & Reprints, 1968, pp. 187-188.

The Sinner's Address to Christ

JOHN MASON

Where lies a sin, I'll drop a tear,
Then view redeeming blood;
To mourning souls Christ will appear,
And surely do them good.
'Tis Thou alone, my Lord, canst give
This aching heart relief;
Christ's gentle voice would make it live,
His hand wipe off my grief.

Those falsely called the sweets of sin
Are bitter unto me;
I loathe the state that I am in,
Lord, may I come to Thee?
But, oh, wilt Thou receive him now
That's coming to Thy door?
For I can bring no dowry, Lord;
I come extremely poor.

What if my tears could make a flood,
My righteousness is dross;
Those tears need washing in Thy blood,
Though wept upon Thy cross.
I have an argument to plead,
Which Thou canst not deny—
Thy grace is free, and Thou dost give
To sinners such as I.

Thou dost invite all wandering souls,
And I am one of those;
With Thee the sick do find a cure,
The weary find repose.
The world and sin will ever vex,
Will trouble and molest;
I therefore trust my soul with Christ,
To bring to heaven's rest.

Mason, John. *Spiritual Songs, or Songs of Praise to Almighty God.*
Edinburgh: James Taylor, 1880, pp. 125-127.

The Branch and the Vine

JOHN FLAVEL

Oh, what considering, serious man can see
The close conjunction of the graft and the tree;
And while he contemplates, he doth not find
This meditation grafted on his mind?

I am the branch, and Christ the vine;
Thy gracious hand did pluck
Me from that native stock of mine,
That I His sap might suck.

The bloody spear did in His heart
A deep incision make,
That grace to me He might impart,
And I therefore partake.

The Spirit and faith are that firm band
Which binds us fast together;
Thus we are clasped, hand in hand,
And nothing can us sever.

Blessed be that hand which did remove
Me from my native place;
This was the wonder of Thy love,
The triumph of Thy grace!
That I, a wild and cursed plant,
Should thus preferred be,
Who all those ornaments do want,
Thou mayest in others see.

As long as ever the root doth live,
The branches are not dry;
While Christ hath grace and life to give,
My soul can never die.

O blessed Savior, never could
A graft cleave to the tree
More close than Thy poor creature would
United be with Thee.

My soul, dishonor not the root,
'Twill be a shame for Thee,
To want the choicest sorts of fruit,
And yet thus grafted be.

Thus you may shake from grafts, before they blow,
More precious fruit than ever trees did grow.

Flavel, John. *The Works of John Flavel.*
London: The Banner of Truth Trust, 1968, V:149-150 (The Poem).

Look Unto Me and Be Ye Saved

JOHN NEWTON

As the serpent raised by Moses
Healed the burning serpent's bite;
Jesus thus Himself discloses
To the wounded sinner's sight.
Hear His gracious invitation,
"I have life and peace to give,
I have wrought out full salvation;

Sinner, look to Me, and live.
Pore upon your sins no longer,
Well I know their mighty guilt;
But My love than death is stronger,
I My blood have freely spilt.
Though your heart has long been hardened,
Look on Me—it soft shall grow;
Past transgressions shall be pardoned,
And I'll wash you white as snow."

"I have seen what you were doing,
Though you little thought of Me;
You were madly bent on ruin,
But I said, 'It shall not be.'
You had been forever wretched,
Had not I espoused your part;
Now behold My arms outstretched
To receive you to My heart."

"Well may shame, and joy, and wonder,
All your inward passions move;
I could crush thee with My thunder,
But I speak to thee in love.
See, your sins are all forgiven,
I have paid the countless sum;
Now My death has opened heaven,
Thither you shall shortly come."

Dearest Savior, we adore Thee
For Thy precious life and death;
Melt each stubborn heart before Thee,
Give us all the eye of faith.
From the law's condemning sentence,
To Thy mercy we appeal;
Thou alone can give repentance,
Thou alone our souls can heal.

Newton, John. *The Works of the Rev. John Newton.*
Edinburgh: Thomas Nelson, 1841, p. 545.

Salvation

ISAAC WATTS

Salvation—oh, the joyful sound!
'Tis pleasure to our ears;
A sovereign balm for every wound,
A cordial for our fears.

Buried in sorrow and in sin,
At hell's dark door we lay;
But we arise by grace divine
To see a heavenly day.

Salvation—let the echo fly,
The spacious earth around;
While all the armies of the sky
Conspire to raise the sound.

Watts, Isaac. *The Psalms and Hymns of Isaac Watts.*
Morgan: Soli Deo Gloria, 1997, p. 465.

Apples of Gold

EDWARD TAYLOR

Apples of gold, in silver pictures shrined,
Enchant the appetite, make mouths to water;
And loveliness in lumps, tuned and enrined.
In jasper cask, when tapped, doth briskly vapor;
Brings forth a birth of keys to unlock love's chest,
That love, like birds, may fly to it from its nest.

Such is my Lord, and more. But what strange thing
Am I become? Sin rusts my lock all over.
Though He ten thousand keys all on a string

Takes out, scarce one is found, unlocks the door;
Which open, my love crinched in a corner lies
Like come shrunk crickling, and scarce can rise.

Lord, open the door, rub off my rust, remove
My sin, and oil my lock (dust there doth shelf).
My wards will trig before the key; my love
Then, as enlivened, leap will on thyself.
It needs must be, that giving hands receive
Again receivers hearts, furled in love wreath.

Unkey my heart; unlock my wardrobe; bring
Out royal robes; adorn my soul, Lord. So,
My love in rich attire shall on my king
Attend, and honor on Him well bestow.
In glory He prepares for His a place,
Whom He doth all beglory here with grace.

He takes them to the shining threshold clear
Of His bright palace, clothed in grace's flame.
Then takes them in thereto, not only there
To have a prospect, but possess the same.
The crown of life, the throne of glory's place,
The Father's house blanched over with orient grace.

Canaan in golden print enwalled with gems;
A kingdom rimmed with glory round; in fine,
A glorious crown paled thick with all the stems
Of grace, and of all properties divine.
How happy wilt Thou make me when these shall
As a blessed heritage unto me fall?

Adorn me, Lord, with holy houswifery;
All blanch my robes with clusters of Thy graces.
Thus lead me to Thy threshold; give mine eye
A peephole there to see bright glories chases.
Then take me in; I'll pay, when I possess
Thy throne, to Thee the rent in happiness.

Taylor, Edward. *The Poetical Works of Edward Taylor.*
Princeton: Princeton Press, 1943, pp. 148-149.

A Closer Walk with God

SANCTIFICATION

I beseech you therefore, brethren,
By the mercies of God,
That you present your bodies a living sacrifice,
Holy, acceptable to God,
Which is your reasonable service.
And do not be conformed to this world,
But be transformed by the renewing of your mind,
That you may prove what is that good and acceptable
and perfect will of God.

— ROMANS 12:1-2

A Closer Walk with God
SANCTIFICATION

"Let not that man think he makes any progress in holiness who walks not over the bellies of his lusts. He who doth not kill sin in his way takes no steps towards his journey's end." (Owen, John. *Temptation and Sin.* Grand Rapids: Sovereign Grace Publishers, 1971, p. 14.)

The journey's beginning is justification, where we stand before God, our Judge, with Christ's righteousness and payment for sin imputed to our record. The journey's end is the believer's glorification, where sin is completely eradicated from our lives. The above quote refers to the journey in between justification and glorification, which is sanctification.

Sanctification is a work of the Holy Spirit in our heart and life where each day we become more like Christ. The power of sin has been broken. As the Westminster Shorter Catechism states: "…we are made more and more able to become dead to sin and alive to righteousness." When we were outside of Christ we were slaves to sin. We had no choice but to sin. Now we have the choice, and we must choose to reject sin as an evidence of our new relationship with God.

Sanctification, however, is not a smooth, downhill walk. To believe we can leave cesspools of iniquity in our lives and simply walk around them is to disregard the teaching of the Scriptures. Those who are able to tolerate sin in their lives will eventually be entrapped and sucked down by this treacherous quicksand. Check with David about the heartbreaking consequences of sin—physically and spiritually. To clean up a cesspool involves long hours of nasty, backbreaking work.

God has given us tools to accomplish this job (Ephesians 6:13-18) and an expert, the Holy Spirit, who enables us. Though painful and hard, this daily repair work must continue. If we are on the right road of a journey that ends with our entrance into glory, we will faithfully labor and sweat in this difficult task.

Walking with God

JOHN NEWTON

Oh, for a closer walk with God,
A calm and heavenly frame;
A light to shine upon the road
That leads me to the Lamb!

Where is the blessedness I knew,
When first I saw the Lord?
Where is the soul-refreshing view
Of Jesus and His Word?

What peaceful hours I once enjoyed!
How sweet their memory still!
But they have left an aching void,
The world can never fill.

Return, O holy Dove, return,
Sweet messenger of rest;
I hate the sins that made Thee mourn,
And drove Thee from my breast.

The dearest idol I have known,
Whate'er that idol be,
Help me to tear it from Thy throne,
And worship only Thee.

So shall my walk be close with God,
Calm and serene my frame;
So purer light shall mark the road,
That leads me to the Lamb.

Newton, John. *The Works of the Rev. John Newton.*
Edinburgh: Thomas Nelson, 1841, p. 526.

The Christian Warfare

SAMUEL STENNETT

My Captain sounds the alarm of war;
Awake, the powers of hell are near!
"To arms! To arms!" I hear Him cry,
'Tis yours to conquer or to die!

Roused by the animating sound,
I cast my eager eyes around;
Make haste to gird my armor on,
And bid each trembling fear be gone.

Hope is my helmet; faith my shield;
Thy Word, my God! the sword I wield;
With sacred truth my loins are girt,
And holy zeal inspires my heart.

Thus armed, I venture on the fight;
Resolved to put my foes to flight;
While Jesus kindly deigns to spread
His conquering banner o'er my head.

In Him I hope; in Him I trust;
His bleeding cross is all my boast.
Through troops of foes He'll lead me on
To victory, and the victor's crown.

Stennett, Samuel. *The Works of Samuel Stennett, D.D.*
London: Thomas Tegg, 1824, pp. 545-546.

The Spiritual Warfare

SAMUEL DAVIES

Arm thee in panoply divine,
My soul, and fired with courage rise;
A thousand enemies combine
To obstruct thy progress to the skies.

Infernal darts perpetual fly,
And scatter various deaths around;
Around thee thousands daily die,
And none escape without a wound.

The world presents her tempting charms,
And wears the aspect of a friend,
Yet, ah, she carries deadly arms,
And all her smiles in ruin end.

But, oh, the flesh, that latent foe,
That treacherous enemy in my breast!
'Tis hence proceeds my overthrow,
And hence I'm conquered by the rest.

Through troops of potent enemies,
Through hostile snares and fields of blood,
If I expect the glorious prize,
I must pursue my dangerous road.

But, ah, how can a feeble worm
Obtain so hard a victory?
Alas, I perish in the storm,
And helpless fall, and bleed, and die.

The glorious prize stands in view,
But deaths and dangers stop my way;
Thou glorious prize! Adieu, adieu!
Here, cruel foes! Come, seize your prey.

But hark, an animating voice,
Majestic breaks from the upper sky,
"Courage, frail worm! Live and rejoice,
I have procured the victory.

"Suspended on the accursed tree,
I crushed the might of all thy foes;
Dying, I spoiled their tyranny,
And triumphed over them when I rose.

"This arm that props the universe,
And holds up nature's tottering frame,
Can all surrounding harms disperse,
And safe protect the feeblest name.

"The Captain of salvation deigns
To lead the van, and guard thy way;
And since thy conquering Leader reigns,
The infernal powers shall miss their prey.

"In Me confide; from Me derive
Courage and strength to keep the field;
In crowds of death then thou shalt live,
And all thy stubborn foes shall yield.

"The Spirit's sword victorious wield,
And steel thy breast with righteousness;
Let faith be thy triumphant shield;
Thy helmet, hope of heav'nly bliss.

"See in My hands the glorious prize;
This crown the conqueror shall wear.
Rise then with dauntless courage rise,
And bid adieu to every fear.

"Though sharp the combat, 'tis but short;
Vict'ry with active wing draws nigh.
And my brave soldiers, all unhurt,
Ere long shall triumph in the sky."

Blessed Jesus, fired with martial zeal,
I arm, and rush into the fight;
And through my weakness still I feel,
I am almighty in Thy might.

Thy gracious Words my heart inspire
With generous zeal for noble deeds;
Let hell and all her hosts appear,
My soul, undaunted, now proceeds.

Satan, affrighted at Thy frown,
Retreats, despairing of his prey;
And all the flatteries earth has shown,
In vain their treacherous charms display.

The flesh, subdued by grace divine,
No more shall triumph o'er the man.
Now, glorious prize, I call thee mine,
Though earth and hell do all they can.

Davies, Samuel. *Collected Poems of Samuel Davies.*
Gainsville: Scholars' Facsimiles & Reprints, 1968, pp. 95-97.

The Good That I Would, I Do Not
(Romans 7:19))

JOHN NEWTON

I would, but cannot sing,
Guilt has untuned my voice;
The serpent's sin-envenomed sting
Has poisoned all my joys.

I know the Lord is nigh,
And would, but cannot pray;
For Satan meets me when I try,
And frights my soul away.

I would, but can't repent,
Though I endeavour oft;
This stony heart can ne'er relent,
Till Jesus make it soft.

I would, but cannot love,
Though wooed by love divine;
No arguments have power to move
A soul so base as mine.

I would, but cannot rest,
In God's most holy will;
I know what He appoints is best,
Yet murmur at it still.

Oh, could I but believe!
Then all would easy be.
I would, but cannot—Lord, relieve;
My help must come from Thee!

But if indeed I would,
Though I can nothing do;
Yet the desire is something good,
For which my praise is due.

By nature prone to ill,
Till Thine appointed hour,
I was as destitute of will,
As now I am of power.

Wilt Thou not crown at length,
The work Thou hast begun?
And with a will, afford me strength,
In all Thy ways to run?

Newton, John. *The Works of the Rev. John Newton.*
Edinburgh: Thomas Nelson, 1841, p. 566.

For Spiritual Protection

JOHN MASON

I have a host of enemies are ever breaking in;
Satan, the world, the flesh devise to ruin me by sin.
I trust to God, as my Defense against their subtleties;
From all destructive baits of sense wilt Thou restrain mine eyes?

Though ye combine against my soul, I make the Lord my guard,
Who will your fiery breath control,who will be my reward.
Whenever dangers near approach, Lord be at hand to me,
And bring my soul by each assault the nearer unto Thee.

Oh, keep from sin, which brings a frown, be gracious at my cry;
Let no temptations cast them down that on Thy grace rely.
Why should that frame set up within which Thine own hand
    did raise,
Be ever broke or slurred by sin? Why shouldst Thou lose
    Thy praise?

Even as Thy care, Thy hand is large, and fills each empty space;
Remember that I am Thy charge; this day consult my case.
My soul, my frame, I will commit to Thee, O Holy Ghost!
Thou art my Guardian, and I trust Thy work shall not be lost.

Mason, John. *Spiritual Songs, or Songs of Praise to Almighty God.*
Edinburgh: James Taylor, 1880, pp. 133-135.

God Insensibly Withdrawn

PHILIP DODDRIDGE

A present God is all our strength,
And all our joy and hope;
When He withdraws, our comforts die,
And every grace must droop.

But flatt'ring trifles charm our hearts
To court their false embrace,
Till justly this neglected Friend
Averts His angry face.

He leaves us, and we miss him not,
But go presumptuous on;
Till baffled, wounded, and enslaved,
We learn that God is gone.

And what, my soul, can then remain,
One ray of light to give?
Severed from Him, their better life,
How can His children live?

Hence, all ye painted forms of joy,
And leave my heart to mourn;
I would devote these eyes to tears,
Till cheered by His return.

Look back, my Lord, and own the place,
Where once Thy temple stood;
For lo, its ruins bear the mark
Of rich atoning blood.

Doddridge, Philip. *The Miscellaneous Works of Philip Doddridge.*
London: Joseph Ogle Robinson, 1830, p. 985.

The Devil Defeated by Faith, Well Fixed and Furnished

RALPH ERSKINE

Be sober, vigilant, and stout;
For every day and hour,
Your foe, the devil, walks about,
Still seeking to devour.

Whom, by a steady faith resist,
In Christ, the Captain's name;
Knowing your fellow-soldiers blessed,
Your warfare is the same.
But may the God, and source of all,
Your grace and warlike store,
Who did by Jesus Christ you call,
To His eternal glore.

After your short while's suff'ring now,
May He perfect you all,
Establish, strengthen, settle you,
Firm like a brazen wall.

To Him whose all-sufficiency,
Alone can thus sustain;
All glory and dominion be
Forevermore. Amen.

Erskine, Ralph. *Erskine's Sermons and Practical Works.*
Aberdeen: A. King & Co., 1863. VII:621.

To the Praise of God for the Forgiveness of Sins

JOHN NORDEN

What shall we do to Thee, O God,
For all that Thou hast done?
Whose love from us removes the rod,
Which our offenses won.

Thy Son hath brought us peace again,
And made us one with Thee;
Although our sins deserved pain,
His cross hath made us free.

Oh, how shall we requite Thy love?
What recompense is due,
To Thee or Him? Help from above,
Our sinful lives renew.

The best reward that we can give,
It helps not Thee at all;
Yet Thou in bounty dost relieve
Us wretched wights in thrall.

Great is Thy glory, love, and might;
Thy mercies have no end.
All thanks and praise to Thee in right
Each heart should still extend.

But we, poor sinners, may cry out
Against ourselves, and say,
"Our purest deeds, like filthy clout,
Our gross conceits bewray."

No stay is in our crooked will;
A rash consent we give
To each delight that seeks to kill
Our souls, wherein we live.

But now Thy saving health extend;
Thy mercies sweet prepare,
And salve our sores; let us amend,
And break Thou Satan's snare.

Norden, John. *A Progress of Piety.*
Cambridge: Cambridge University Press, 1968, pp. 63-64.

Thy Maker Is Thy Husband

RALPH ERSKINE

Of light and life, of grace and glore,
In Christ thou art partaker,
Rejoice in Him forevermore,
Thy Husband is thy Maker.

He made thee, yea, made thee His bride,
Nor heeds thine ugly patch;
To what He made He'll still abide,
Thy Husband made the match.

He made all, yea, He made all thine,
All to thee shall be given.
Who can thy kingdom undermine?
Thy Husband made the heaven.

What earthly thing can thee annoy?
He made the earth to be;
The waters cannot thee destroy,
Thy Husband made the sea.

Don't fear the flaming element
Thee hurt with burning ire,
Or that the scorching heart torment;
Thy Husband made the fire.

Infectious streams shall ne'er destroy,
While He is pleased to spare;
Thou shalt thy vital breath enjoy,
Thy Husband made the air.

The sun that guides the golden day,
The moon that rules the night,
The starry frame, the Milky Way,
Thy Husband made for light.

The bird that wings its airy path,
The fish that cuts the flood,
The creeping crowd that swarms beneath,
Thy Husband made for good.

The grazing herd, the beasts of prey,
The creatures great and small,
For thy behoof their tribute pay;
Thy Husband made them all.

Thine's Paul, Apollos, life and death,
Things present, things to be;
And everything that being hath,
Thy Husband made for thee.

In Tophet, where the damned resort,
Thy soul shall never dwell,
Nor needs from thence imagine hurt;
Thy Husband formed hell.

Satan with instruments of his,
May rage, yet dread no evil;
So far as he a creature is,
Thy Husband made the devil.

His black temptations may afflict,
His fiery darts annoy;
But all his works, and hellish tricks,
Thy Husband will destroy.

Let armies strong of earthly gods,
Combine with hellish ghosts,
They live or languish, at His nods;
Thy Husband's Lord of hosts.

What can thee hurt? Whom dost thou fear?
All things are at His call.
Thy Maker is thy Husband dear,
Thy Husband all in all.

What dost thou seek? What dost thou want?
He'll thy desires fulfill;
He gave Himself; what won't He grant?
Thy Husband's at thy will.

The more thou dost of Him desire,
The more He loves to give;
High let thy mounting aims aspire,
Thy Husband gives thee leave.

The less thou seekest, the less thou dost
His bounty set on high;
But highest seekers here do most
Thy Husband glorify.

Wouldst thou have grace? Well, but 'tis meet,
He should more glory gain.
Wouldst thou have Father, Son, and Spirit?
Thy Husband say, "Amen."

He'll kindly act the liberal God,
Devising liberal things;
With royal gifts His subjects load;
Thy Husband's King of kings.

No earthly monarch has such store,
As thou hast e'en in hand;
But, oh, how infinitely more
Thy Husband gives on band.

Thou hast indeed the better part,
The part will fail thee never.
Thy Husband's hand, thy Husband's heart,
Thy Husband's all forever.

Erskine, Ralph. *Erskine's Sermons and Practical Works.*
Aberdeen: A. King & Co., 1863. VII:161-163.

The Prince of Darkness Defeated

MATTHEW HALE

The prince of darkness, flushed with victory,
In our first parents' first apostasy,
Usurped a lawless sovereignty on man,
Revolted thus from his first Sovereign.

And thought by that apostasy he found,
Under the chains of death, his vassal bound,
Yet to secure his empire, he o'erspread
The world with darkness, and thereby did lead

His captives as he pleased. Thus he bears
His rule usurped near four thousand years;
Except some small confined plantation,
Within a family or a nation.

But now to put a period to this reign,
Of this usurper, and reduce again,
Man to his just subjection, 'tis decreed
That man from this subjection shall be freed;

And this too by the absolute command
Of an immediate power, nor shall the bands
Of angels, glorious hosts, engaged be,
To rescue man from this captivity.

But God an unsuspected means intends,
And yet most suitable unto this end;
Sin stained our nature, and the serpent's wile,
Did man of innocence and life beguile.

By Man his head is crushed; the lawful Lord
Unto His creature man to his life restored;
A virgin's Son is born—this rising sun,
The world's enthralling darkness overruns.

A Child to us is born, whose innocence
Our nature's spot and stain doth purge and cleanse;
His wounds, our cure; His bonds, our liberty;
His death becomes our life, our victory.

And this is He whose birth we celebrate,
And from this day our happiness do date.

Hale, Matthew. *Contemplations, Moral and Divine.*
London: Sherwood, Neely, & Jones, n.d., II:592.

Jesus, Thy Light Impart

AUGUSTUS TOPLADY

Jesus, Thy light impart,
And lead me in Thy path;
I have an unbelieving heart,
But Thou canst give me faith.

The work in me fulfil,
Which mercy hath begun;
I have a proud rebellious will,
But Thou canst melt it down.

Sin on my heart is wrote,
I am throughout impure;
But my disease, O Lord, is not
Too hard for Thee to cure.

The darkness of my mind
Lies open to Thy sight;
Jesus, I am by nature blind,
But Thou canst give me light.

Send down Thy Holy Ghost,
To cleanse and fill with peace;
For oh, mine inward parts thou knowest
Are very wickedness.

Thy love all power hath,
Its power in me exert;
And give me living, active faith,
That purifies the heart.

Unrivaled reign within,
My only Sovereign be,
Oh, crucify the man of sin,
And form Thyself in me.

Thy blood's renewing might,
Can make the foulest clean;
Can wash the Ethiopian white,
And change the leopard's skin.

That, Lord, can bring me nigh,
And wipe my sins away;
Can lift my abject soul on high,
And call me into day.

Fulfill Thy gracious Word,
And show my guilt forgiv'n;
Bid me embrace my dying Lord,
And mount with Him to heaven.

Toplady, Augustus. *The Works of Augustus Toplady.*
London: J. Chidley. 1837, p. 890 (Poem XXIII)

The Conflict

JOHN MASON

Oh, what a war is in my soul, which fain would be devout!
I am most weary with the fight, but may not yet give out.
The flesh and spirit both contend for this weak soul of mine,
That oft I know not what to do; but, Lord, I would be Thine.

I would believe, but unbelief prevails the other way;
And I have constant cause of grief, a longer night than day.
I cry to God; those cries declare whose part my soul does take;
Accept my poor desires while I do this resistance make.

My evidences should be clear; but, ah, the blots of sin
Turn cheering hope to saddening fear and make black doubts
  within.
The laws of sin and grace will jar both dwelling in one room,
The saints expect perpetual war till ye are sent for home.

Although these combats make you fear they should not cast
  you down;
God will give grace to hold out here, and glory for its crown.

Mason, John. *Spiritual Songs, or Songs of Praise to Almighty God.*
Edinburgh: James Taylor, 1880, pp. 137-138

A Living and a Dead Faith

ISAAC WATTS

Mistaken souls, that dream of heaven,
And make their empty boast
Of inward joys, and sins forgiven,
While they are slaves to lust!

Vain are our fancies, airy flights,
If faith be cold and dead;
None but a living power unites
To Christ the living Head.

'Tis faith that changes all the heart;
'Tis faith that works by love;
That bids all sinful joys depart
And lifts the thoughts above.

'Tis faith that conquers earth and hell
By a celestial power;
This is the grace that shall prevail
In the decisive hour.

Faith must obey her Father's will
As well as trust His grace;
A pardoning God is jealous still
For His own holiness.

When from the curse He sets us free,
He makes our natures clean;
Nor would He send His Son to be
The minister of sin.

His Spirit purifies our frame
And seals our peace with God;
Jesus and His salvation came,
By water and by blood.

Watts, Isaac. *The Psalms and Hymns of Isaac Watts.*
Morgan: Soli Deo Gloria Publications, 1997, pp. 388-389.

Thirsting
for the Heavenly

EXCELLENCY OF CHRIST

As the deer pants for the water brooks,
So pants my soul for Thee, O God.
My soul thirsts for God, for the living God.
— PSALM 42:1-2

Thirsting for the Heavenly
EXCELLENCY OF CHRIST

"Tell some that they must add faith to faith, one degree of grace to another, and you will find them having a mind more to join house to house and field to field. They thirst, but for what? Is it to have more of Christ, or more of earth? Some think they never have enough until death comes and stops their mouth with a shovel full of dirt taken from their own grave. How tormenting it must be to be always crying for more weight, yet never having enough to crush their covetous desire. If men but would believe it, the only way to quench thirst for the things of this world is to enkindle a thirst for Christ and Heaven." (Gurnall, William. *The Christian in Complete Armor.* Layfayette, Ind: Sovereign Grace Trust Fund, 1989, p. 20.)

Again and again we are told that temporal things will never satisfy, that we cheat ourselves by settling for the play things of this world. So why is it that we have such a hard time displacing from our hearts the love of them and are continually trying to satisfy our deepest longings with "more earth"?

To displace our affections from one object, we must have another shown us of higher worth. The soul of man will not release an object of affection thus leaving a void, a negative and cheerless vacancy in it. God has created us in such a way that we are miserable if we possess a capacity of desire without having the object of that desire.

The wrong affections that control us will only be left behind when the soul is made to realize that it is the triune God who is more excellent and far more worthy of its attachment than the trifles of this world. Thus the void left by releasing them is replaced by an object of higher worth.

This is the reason why it is important to show the excellencies of Christ, continually to woo men to Christ, for then they will exchange a lesser good for a greater. Once we have been given a taste of the Living Water, the things of this world will suddenly leave a dry taste in our mouths.

Drink and Live

JOHN NEWTON

Not to Sinai's dreadful blaze,
But to Zion's throne of grace,
By a way marked out with blood,
Sinners now approach to God

Not to hear the fiery law,
But with humble joy to draw
Water, by that well supplied,
Jesus opened when He died.

Lord, there are no streams but Thine,
Can assuage a thirst like mine;
'Tis a thirst Thyself didst give,
Let me, therefore, drink and live.

Newton, John. *The Works of the Rev. John Newton.*
Edinburgh: Thomas Nelson, 1841, p. 632.

The Excellencies of Christ

SAMUEL STENNETT

To Christ, the Lord, let every tongue
Its noblest tribute bring;
When He's the subject of the song,
Who can refuse to sing?

Survey the beauties of His face,
And on His glories dwell;
Think of the wonders of His grace,
And all His triumphs tell.

Majestic sweetness sits enthroned
Upon His awful brow;
His head with radiant glories crowned,
His lips with grace o'erflow.

No mortal can with Him compare,
Among the sons of men;
Fairer He is than all the fair,
That fill the heavenly train.

He saw me plunged in deep distress,
He flew to my relief;
For me He bore the shameful cross,
And carried all my grief.

His hand a thousand blessings pours
Upon my guilty head;
His presence gilds my darkest hours,
And guards my sleeping bed.

To Him I owe my life, and breath,
And all the joys I have;
He makes me triumph over death,
And saves me from the grave.

To heaven, the place of His abode,
He brings my weary feet;
Shows me the glories of my God,
And makes my joys complete.

Since from His bounty I receive
Such proofs of love divine,
Had I a thousand hearts to give,
Lord, they should all be thine!

Stennett, Samuel. *The Works of Samuel Stennett, D.D.*
London: Thomas Tegg, 1824, pp. 539-540

Thanksgiving for the Righteousness of Christ
AUGUSTUS TOPLADY

Fountain of never-ceasing grace, Thy saints' exhaustless theme,
Great object of immortal praise, essentially supreme;
We bless Thee for the glorious fruits Thy incarnation gives;
The righteousness which grace imputes, and faith alone receives.

Whom heav'n's angelic host adores was slaughtered for our sin;
The guilt, O Lord, was wholly ours, the punishment was Thine.
Our God in flesh, to set us free, was manifested here;
And meekly bare our sins, that we His righteousness might wear.

Imputatively guilty then our Substitute was made,
That we the blessings might obtain for which His blood was shed:
Himself He offered on the cross our sorrows to remove;
And all He suffered was for us, and all He did was love.

In Him we have a righteousness by God Himself approved
Our Rock, our sure Foundation this which never can be moved.
Our ransom by His death He paid, for all His people giv'n,
The law He perfectly obeyed that they might enter heav'n.

As all, when Adam sinned alone, in his transgression died,
So by the righteousness of One are sinners justified,
We to Thy merit, gracious Lord, with humblest joy submit,
Again to paradise restored, in Thee alone complete.

Our souls His watchful love retrieves, nor lets them go astray,
His righteousness to us He gives, and takes our sins away.
We claim salvation in His right, adopted and forgiven,
His merit is our robe of light, His death the gate of heaven.

Toplady, Augustus. *The Works of Augustus Toplady.*
London: J. Chidley, 1837, pp. 897-898.

The Description of Christ the Beloved

ISAAC WATTS

The wondering world inquires to know
Why I should love my Jesus so;
"What are His charms," say they, "above
The objects of a mortal love?"

Yes, my Beloved, to my sight,
Shows a sweet mixture, red and white;
All human beauties, all divine,
In my Beloved meet and shine.

White is His soul, from blemish free;
Red with the blood He shed for me;
The fairest of ten thousand fairs;
A sun among ten thousand stars.

His head the finest gold excels;
There wisdom in perfection dwells,
And glory like a crown adorns
Those temples once beset with thorns.

Compassions in His heart are found,
Hard by the signals of his wound;
His scarred side no more shall bear
The cruel scourge, the piercing spear.

His hands are fairer to behold
Than diamonds set in rings of gold;
Those heavenly hands, that on the tree
Were nailed, and torn, and bled for me!

Though once He bowed His feeble knees,
Loaded with sins and agonies,
Now on the throne of His command
His legs like marble pillars stand.

His eyes are majesty and love,
The eagle tempered with the dove;
No more shall trickling sorrows roll
Through those dear windows of His soul.

His mouth, that poured out long complaints,
Now smiles and cheers His fainting saints;
His countenance more graceful is
Than Lebanon with all its trees.

All over glorious is my Lord;
Must be beloved, and yet adored;
His worth if all the nations knew,
Sure the whole earth would love Him too.

Watts, Isaac. *The Psalms and Hymns of Isaac Watts.*
Morgan: Soli Deo Gloria Publications, 1997, pp. 350-351.

Recovered from the Tomb

MATHER BYLES

To Thee, my Lord, I lift the song,
Awake, my tuneful powers;
In constant praise my grateful tongue
Shall fill my following hours.

Guilty, condemned, undone I stood;
I bid my God depart.
He took my sins, and paid His blood,
And turned this wandering heart.z

Death, the grim tyrant, seized my frame,
Vile, loathsome and accursed;
His breath renews the vital flame,
And glories change the dust.

Now, Savior, shall Thy praise commence;
My soul by Thee brought home,
And every member, every sense,
Recovered from the tomb.

To Thee my reason I submit,
My love, my memory, Lord,
My eyes to read, my hands to write,
My lips to preach Thy Word.

Byles, Mather. *Mather Byles' Works.*
Delmar: Scholars' Facsimiles & Reprints, 1978, pp. 17-18
("An Hymn to Christ for Our Regeneration and Resurrection").

My Soul Thirsts for God

JOHN NEWTON

I thirst, but not as once I did,
The vain delights of earth to share;
Thy wounds, Emmanuel, all forbid
That I should seek my pleasures there.

It was the sight of Thy dear cross,
First weaned my soul from earthly things;
And taught me to esteem as dross,
The mirth of fools and pomp of kings.

I want that grace that springs from Thee,
That quickens all things where it flows,
And makes a wretched thorn like me,
Bloom as the myrtle, or the rose.

Dear fountain of delight unknown!
No longer sink below the brim;
But overflow, and pour me down,
A living and life-giving stream!

For sure, of all the plants that share
The notice of Thy Father's eye,
None proves less grateful to His care,
Or yields Him meaner fruit than I.

Newton, John. *The Works of the Rev. John Newton.*
Edinburgh: Thomas Nelson, 1841, pp. 623-624.

Christ the Beloved

SAMUEL DAVIES

Let others let their passions rove
Round all the earth, from shore to shore;
Since Jesus is my friend and love,
My utmost wish can grasp no more.

His glories have allured my eye,
And into love transformed my heart;
To Him my tenderest passions fly;
Jesus, nor shall they e'er depart.

Upon His friendship I rely,
Still of His tender care secure;
My wants are all before His eye!
Nor can they overcome His pow'r.

His presence fills unbounded space;
My heavenly friend is always nigh.
Full of compassion, rich in grace;
Touched with the tenderest sympathy.

Faithful and constant is His love,
And my ungrateful conduct hides;
Safe to the happy world above,
The meanest of His friends He guides.

Amid the agonies of death,
And terrors of the final doom,
He saves them from almighty wrath,
And leads the helpless pilgrims home.

Oh, may an everlasting flame
Of love possess my grateful mind!
And my last breath adore His name,
Who condescends to be my friend!

Davies, Samuel. *Collected Poems of Samuel Davies.*
Gainsville: Scholars' Facsimiles & Reprints, 1968, pp. 94-95.

A Friend That Sticks Closer Than a Brother

JOHN NEWTON

One there is, above all others,
Well deserves the name of Friend;
His is love beyond a brother's,
Costly, free, and knows no end;
They who once His kindness prove,
Find it everlasting love.

Which of all our friends to save us,
Could or would have shed their blood?
But our Jesus died to have us
Reconciled to Him in God;
This was boundless love indeed.
Jesus is a friend in need.

Men, when raised to lofty stations,
Often know their friends no more;
Slight and scorn their poor relations,

Though they valued them before;
But our Savior always owns
Those whom He redeemed with groans.

When He lived on earth abased,
Friend of sinners was His name;
Now above all glory raised,
He rejoices in the same:
Still He calls them brethren, friends,
And to all their wants attends.

Could we bear from one another
What He daily bears from us?
Yet this glorious Friend and Brother
Loves us though we treat Him thus;
Though for good we render ill,
He accounts us brethren still.

Oh, for grace our hearts to soften!
Teach us, Lord, at length to love;
We, alas, forget too often,
What a Friend we have above;
But when home our souls are brought,
We will love Thee as we ought.

Newton, John. *The Works of the Rev. John Newton.*
Edinburgh: Thomas Nelson, 1841, p. 542.

The Refuge, River, and Rock of the Church

JOHN NEWTON

He who on earth as man was known,
And bore our sins and pains,
Now seated on th'eternal throne,
The God of glory reigns.

His hands the wheels of nature guide,
With an unerring skill;
And countless worlds, extended wide,
Obey His sovereign will.

While harps unnumbered sound His praise,
In yonder world above;
His saints on earth admire His ways,
And glory in His love.

His righteousness to faith revealed,
Wrought out for guilty worms,
Affords a hiding place and shield
From enemies and storms.

This land, through which His pilgrims go,
Is desolate and dry;
But streams of grace from Him o'erflow
Their thirst to satisfy.

When troubles, like a burning sun,
Beat heavy on their head,
To this Almighty Rock they run,
And find a pleasing shade.

How glorious He, how happy they,
In such a glorious Friend!
Whose love secures them all the way,
And crowns them at the end.

Newton, John. *The Works of the Rev. John Newton.*
Edinburgh: Thomas Nelson, 1841, p. 544.

Christ Our Wisdom and Righteousness

ISAAC WATTS

Buried in shadows of the night,
We lie till Christ restores the light;
Wisdom descends to heal the blind,
And chase the darkness of the mind.

Our guilty souls are drowned in tears,
Till His atoning blood appears;
Then we awake from deep distress,
And sing, "The Lord our Righteousness."

Our very frame is mixed with sin,
His Spirit makes our natures clean;
Such virtues from His sufferings flow,
At once to cleanse and pardon too.

Jesus beholds where Satan reigns,
Binding his slaves in heavy chains;
He sets the prisoners free, and breaks
The iron bondage from our necks.

Poor helpless worms in Thee possess
Grace, wisdom, pow'r, and righteousness;
Thou art our Mighty All, and we,
Give our whole selves, O Lord, to Thee.

Watts, Isaac. *The Psalms and Hymns of Isaac Watts.*
Morgan: Soli Deo Gloria Publications, 1997, p. 364.

Names of Christ Expressive of His Offices

AUGUSTUS TOPLADY

Low at Thy feet, O Christ, we fall,
Enabled to confess,
And call Thee by the Holy Ghost,
The Lord our Righteousness.

God over all, Immanuel reigns,
With His great Father one;
The brightness of His glory Thou,
And partner of His throne.

Author and Finisher of faith,
In all that know Thy name,
A lion to Thy stubborn foes,
But to Thy friends a lamb.

Scepter of Israel, Prince of Peace,
Immortal King of kings;
The Sun of Righteousness, that shines
With healing in His wings.

The gift of God to fallen man,
The Lord of quick and dead;
A well of life to fainting souls,
And their sustaining bread.

Foundation of Thy people's joy,
Their pardon and their rest;
On earth our sacrifice for sin,
In heaven our great High Priest.

The Lord of life who suffered death
That we might heav'n regain;
The source of blessing, who on earth,
Was made a curse for man.

Was poor that Adam's needy sons,
Treasure in Thee might find;
Repairer of the dreadful breach,
Restorer of mankind.

Through Thy desert a fallen race,
To God may gain access;
With Thy fine linen deck our souls,
Thy perfect righteousness.

With that celestial robe endued,
We every foe defy;
On earth it shall our armor be,
Our glory in the sky.

Toplady, Augustus. *The Works of Augustus Toplady.*
London: J. Chidley, 1837, p. 899.

The Offices of Christ

ISAAC WATTS

Join all the names of love and power,
That ever men or angels bore,
All are too mean to speak His worth,
Or set Immanuel's glory forth.

But oh, what condescending ways,
He takes to teach His heavenly grace!
My eyes with joy and wonder see
What forms of love He bears for me.

The Angel of the cov'nant stands
With His commission in His hands,
Sent from His Father's milder throne,
To make the great salvation known.

Great Prophet, let me bless Thy name;
By Thee the joyful tidings came,
Of wrath appeased, of sins forgiv'n,
Of hell subdued, and peace with heav'n.

My bright example and my guide,
I would be walking near Thy side;
Oh, let me never run astray,
Nor follow the forbidden way!

I love my Shepherd, He shall keep
My wandering soul among His sheep;
He feeds His flock, He calls their names,
And in His bosom bears the lambs.

My Surety undertakes my cause,
Answ'ring His Father's broken laws;
Behold my soul at freedom set,
My Surety paid the dreadful debt.

Jesus, my great High Priest, has died;
I seek no sacrifice beside;
His blood did once for all atone,
And now it pleads before the throne.

My Advocate appears on high,
The Father lays his thunder by;
Not all that earth or hell can say
Shall turn my Father's heart away.

My Lord, my Conqueror, and my King!
Thy scepter and Thy sword I sing;
Thine is the vict'ry, and I sit
A joyful subject at Thy feet.

Aspire, my soul, to glorious deeds,
Thy Captain of salvation leads;
March on, nor fear to win the day,
Though death and hell obstruct the way.

Should death, and hell, and pow'rs unknown,
Put all their forms of mischief on,
I shall be safe; for Christ displays
Salvation in more sovereign ways.

Watts, Isaac. *The Psalms and Hymns of Isaac Watts.*
Morgan: Soli Deo Gloria Publications, 1997, pp. 398-399.

Bitter and Sweet

JOHN NEWTON

Kindle, Savior, in my heart,
A flame of love divine;
Hear, for mine I trust Thou art,
And sure I would be Thine.
If my soul has felt Thy grace,
If to me Thy name is known,
Why should trifles fill the place
Due to Thyself alone?

'Tis a strange mysterious life
I live from day to day;
Light and darkness, peace and strife,
Bear an alternate sway.
When I think the battle won,
I have to fight it o'er again;
When I say I'm overthrown,
Relief I soon obtain.

Often at the mercy seat,
While calling on Thy name,
Swarms of evil thoughts I meet,
Which fill my soul with shame;
Agitated in my mind,
Like a feather in the air,
Can I thus a blessing find?
My soul, can this be prayer?

But when Christ, my Lord and Friend,
Is pleased to show His power;
All at once my troubles end,
And I've a golden hour.
Then I see His smiling face,
Feel the pledge of joys to come;
Often, Lord, repeat this grace,
Till Thou shalt call me home.

Newton, John. *The Works of the Rev. John Newton.*
Edinburgh: Thomas Nelson, 1841, p. 613.

True Happiness

JOHN NEWTON

Fix my heart and eyes on Thine!
What are other objects worth?
But to see Thy glory shine,
Is a heaven begun on earth.
Trifles can no longer move;
Oh, I tread on all beside,
When I feel my Savior's love,
And remember how He died!

Now my search is at an end,
Now my wishes rove no more!
Thus my moments I would spend,
Love, and wonder, and adore.
Jesus, source of excellence!
All Thy glorious love reveal!
Kingdoms shall not bribe me hence,
While this happiness I feel.

Take my heart, 'tis all Thine own,
To Thy will my spirit frame;
Thou shalt reign, and Thou alone,
Over all I have or am.

If a foolish thought shall dare
To rebel against Thy Word,
Slay it, Lord, and do not spare,
Let it feel Thy Spirit's sword!

Making thus the Lord my choice,
I have nothing more to choose,
But to listen to Thy voice,
And my will in Thine to lose;
Thus, whatever may betide,
I shall safe and happy be,
Still content and satisfied,
Having all in having Thee.

Newton, John. *The Works of the Rev. John Newton.*
Edinburgh: Thomas Nelson, 1841, p. 625

Characters of Christ

ISAAC WATTS

Go, worship at Emmanuel's feet,
See in His face what wonders meet!
Earth is too narrow to express
His worth, His glory, or His grace.

The whole creation can afford,
But some faint shadows of my Lord;
Nature, to make His beauties known,
Must mingle colors not her own.

Is He compared to wine or bread?
Dear Lord, our souls would thus be fed;
That flesh, that dying blood of Thine,
Is bread of life, is heavenly wine.

Is He a tree? The world receives
Salvation from His healing leaves;
That righteous branch, that fruitful bough,
Is David's root and offspring too.

Is He a rose? Not Sharon yields
Such fragrancy in all her fields;
Or if the lily He assume,
The valleys bless the rich perfume.

Is He a vine? His heavenly root
Supplies the boughs with life and fruit;
Oh, let a lasting union join
My soul the branch to Christ the vine!

Is He the Head? Each member lives,
And owns the vital powers He gives;
The saints below and saints above
Joined by His Spirit and His love.

Is He a fountain? There I bathe,
And heal the plague of sin and death;
These waters all my soul renew,
And cleanse my spotted garments too.

Is He a fire? He'll purge my dross;
But the true gold sustains no loss;
Like a refiner shall He sit,
And tread the refuse with His feet.

Is He a rock? How firm He proves!
The Rock of Ages never moves;
Yet the sweet streams that from Him flow,
Attend us all the desert through.

Is He a way? He leads to God,
The path is drawn in lines of blood;
There would I walk with hope and zeal,
Till I arrive at Zion's hill.

Is He a door? I'll enter in;
Behold the pastures large and green,
A paradise divinely fair;
None but the sheep have freedom there.

Is He designed the Cornerstone,
For men to build their heaven upon?
I'll make Him my foundation too,
Nor fear the plots of hell below.

Is He a temple? I adore
The indwelling majesty and power;
And still to this most holy place,
Whenever I pray, I turn my face.

Is He a star? He breaks the night.
Piercing the shades with dawning light;
I know His glories from afar,
I know the Bright, the Morning Star.

Is He a sun? His beams are grace,
His course is joy and righteousness;
Nations rejoice when He appears,
To chase their clouds and dry their tears.

Oh, let me climb those higher skies,
Where storms and darkness never rise!
There He displays His power abroad,
And shines and reigns the incarnate God.

Nor earth, nor seas, nor sun, nor stars,
Nor heaven, His full resemblance bears;
His beauties we can never trace,
Till we behold Him face to face.

Watts, Isaac. *The Psalms and Hymns of Isaac Watts.*
Morgan: Soli Deo Gloria Publications, 1997, pp. 393-395

Praise to the Redeemer

JOHN NEWTON

Prepare a thankful song
To the Redeemer's name!
His praises should employ each tongue,
And every heart inflame!

He laid His glory by,
And dreadful pains endured,
That rebels, such as you and I,
From wrath might be secured.

Upon the cross He died,
Our debt of sin to pay;
The blood and water from His side
Wash guilt and filth away.

And now He pleading stands,
For us, before the throne,
And answers all the law's demands
With what Himself hath done.

He sees us, willing slaves,
To sin, and Satan's power;
But, with an outstretched arm, He saves,
In His appointed hour.

The Holy Ghost He sends,
Our stubborn souls to move,
To make His enemies His friends,
And conquer them by love.

The love of sin departs,
The life of grace takes place,
Soon as His voice invites our hearts,
To rise and seek His face.

The world and Satan rage,
But He their power controls;
His wisdom, love, and truth, engage
Protection for our souls.

Though pressed, we will not yield,
But shall prevail at length;
For Jesus is our sun and shield,
Our righteousness and strength.

Assured that Christ, our King,
Will put our foes to flight,
We on the field of battle sing,
And triumph while we fight.

Newton, John. *The Works of the Rev. John Newton.*
Edinburgh: Thomas Nelson, 1841, p. 631.

JOHN NEWTON

Why should I fear the darkest hour,
Or tremble at the tempter's pow'r?
Jesus vouchsafes to be my tow'r.

Though hot the fight, why quit the field?
Why must I either flee or yield,
Since Jesus is my mighty shield?

When creature-comforts fade and die,
Worldlings may weep, but why should I?
Jesus still lives, and still is nigh.

Though all the flocks and herds were dead,
My soul a famine need not dread,
For Jesus is my living bread.

I know not what may soon betide,
Or how my wants shall be supplied;
But Jesus knows and will provide.

Though sin would fill me with distress,
The throne of grace I dare address,
For Jesus is my righteousness.

Though faint my prayers, and cold my love,
My steadfast hope shall not remove,
While Jesus intercedes above.

Against me earth and hell combine,
But on my side is pow'r divine;
Jesus is all, and He is mine.

Newton, John. *The Works of the Rev. John Newton.*
Edinburgh: Thomas Nelson, 1841, p. 619.

The Helm of the Heart

RELIGIOUS AFFECTIONS

And now, Israel, what does the Lord require of you,
But to fear the Lord your God,
To walk in all His ways and to love Him,
To serve the Lord your God with all your heart
and with all your soul, and to keep the commandments
of the Lord and His statutes which I command you today
for your good?

— DEUTERONOMY 10:12-13

The Helm of the Heart
RELIGIOUS AFFECTIONS

"Affections are in the soul as the helm in the ship; if it be laid hold on by a skillful hand, he turneth the whole vessel which way he pleaseth. If God hath the powerful hand of his grace upon our affections, he turns our soul to a compliance with his institutions, instructions, afflictions, trials, and all sorts of providences, and in mercy holds them firm against all winds and storms of temptations, that they shall not hurry them on pernicious dangers. Such a soul alone is tractable and pliable to all intimations of God's will." (Owen, John. *The Grace and Duty of Being Spiritually Minded.* Grand Rapids: Baker Book House, 1977, p. 222.)

The mere presentation of truth is not enough to bring the heart into compliance with it. We may know the truth and yet not do it. Or even worse, we may modify our behavior and do what we have been told is pleasing to God, but our religion stays on the surface and never gets to the heart. We quite unwittingly become formalists and hypocrites by doing such, for God asks for our affections and He desires them above all else.

God seeks more than behavior modification. All God's gracious dealings with His children have this aim: to recover the affections of man to Himself. A heart set on fire with love and gratitude to God is the motivation He seeks for our obedience.

Watch carefully what you find satisfaction in and whom you rest on, for that it is which is steering the helm of your ship. "As a person thinks in his heart, so he is" (Proverbs 23:7). "For where your treasure is, there will your heart be also" (Matthew 6:21). Let the skillful hands of God lay hold of your helm (affections) and trust Him to safely steer your vessel through the storms of life.

The Victor of My Heart

RALPH ERSKINE

Let Him who in my room and place,
Did act the kindest part—
The God of love, and Prince of peace,
The Victor of my heart.

With sweet endearments from above,
Let Him my soul embrace;
To show my interest in His love,
And manifest His grace,

With blessings of Thy mouth divine,
Oh, may I favored be!
More precious is Thy love than wine,
More sweet than life to me.

I was among the traitorous crew,
Doomed to eternal fire,
When He, to pay the ransom, flew
On wings of strong desire.

Jesus the God, with naked arms,
Hangs on a cross and dies.
Then mounts the throne, with mighty charms,
To embrace me from the skies.

His mouth delicious, heaven reveals;
His kisses from above
Are pardons, promises, and seals
Of everlasting love.

Erskine, Ralph. *Erskine's Sermons and Practical Works.*
Aberdeen: A. King & Co., 1863, VII:313-314.

True Pleasures

JOHN NEWTON

Lord, my soul with pleasure springs,
When Jesus' name I hear,
And when God the Spirit brings
The Word of promise near;

Beauties, too, in holiness,
Still delighted I perceive;
Nor have words that can express
The joy Thy precepts give.

Clothed in sanctity and grace,
How sweet it is to see
Those who love Thee as they pass,
Or whom they wait on thee!

Pleasant too, to sit and tell,
What we owe to love divine,
Till our bosoms grateful swell,
And eyes begin to shine.

Those the comforts I possess,
Which God shall still increase;
All His ways are pleasantness,
And all His paths are peace.

Nothing Jesus did or spoke,
Henceforth let me ever slight;
For I love His easy yoke,
And find His burden light.

Newton, John. *The Works of the Rev. John Newton.*
Edinburgh: Thomas Nelson, 1841, p. 620.

My Meditations of Him Shall Be Sweet

AUGUSTUS TOPLADY

When languor and disease invade
This trembling house of clay,
'Tis sweet to look beyond our cage,
And long to fly away.

Sweet to look inward and attend
The whispers of His love;
Sweet to look upward to the place
Where Jesus pleads above.

Sweet to look back and see my name
In life's fair book set down;
Sweet to look forward and behold
Eternal joys my own.

Sweet to reflect how grace divine
My sins on Jesus laid;
Sweet to remember that His blood
My debt of suff'rings paid.

Sweet on His righteousness to stand,
Which saves from second death;
Sweet to experience day by day,
His Spirit's quick'ning breath.

Sweet on His faithfulness to rest,
Whose love can never end;
Sweet on His covenant of grace,
For all things to depend.

Sweet in the confidence of faith,
To trust His firm decrees;
Sweet to lie passive in His hand,
And know no will but His.

Sweet to rejoice in lively hope,
That, when my change shall come,
Angels will hover round my bed,
And waft my spirit home.

There shall my disimprisoned soul
Behold Him and adore;
Be with His likeness satisfied,
And grieve and sin no more.

Shall see Him wear that very flesh
On which my guilt was lain;
His love intense, His merit fresh,
As though but newly slain.

Soon too my slumbering dust shall hear
The trumpet's quickening sound;
And, by my Savior's power rebuilt,
At His right hand be found.

There eyes shall see him in that day,
The God that died for me;
And all my rising bones shall say,
Lord, who is like to Thee?

If such the views which grace unfolds,
Weak as it is below,
What raptures must the Church above
In Jesus' presence know!

If such the sweetness of the stream,
What must the fountain be,
Where saints and angels draw their bliss
Immediately from Thee.

Oh, may the unctions of these truths,
Forever with me stay;
Till from her sinful cage dismissed
My spirit flies away.

Toplady, Augustus. *The Works of Augustus Toplady.*
London: J. Chidley. 1837, p. 915.

Pleading with God under Affliction

SAMUEL STENNETT

Why should a living man complain
Of deep distress within,
Since every sigh, and every pain,
Is but the fruit of sin?

No, Lord, I'll patiently submit,
Nor ever dare rebel;
Yet sure I may, here at Thy feet,
My painful feelings tell.

Thou seest what floods of sorrow rise,
And beat upon my soul;
Our trouble to another cries,
Billows on billows roll.

From fear to hope, and hope to fear,
My shipwrecked soul is tossed;
Till I am tempted in despair
To give up all for lost.

Yet through the stormy clouds I'll look
Once more to Thee my God!
Oh, fix my feet upon a rock,
Beyond the gaping flood.

One look of mercy from Thy face
Will set my heart at ease;
One all-commanding word of grace
Will make the tempest cease.

Stennett, Samuel. *The Works of Samuel Stennett, D.D.*
London: Printed for Thomas Tegg, 1824, pp. 546-547.

Lord, Save Us

AUGUSTUS TOPLADY

Pilot of the soul, awake,
Save us for Thy mercies' sake;
Now rebuke the angry deep,
Save, oh, save Thy sinking ship!

Stand at the helm, our vessel steer;
Mighty on our side appear.
Savior, teach us to decry,
Where the rocks and quicksands lie.

The waves shall impotently roll,
If Thou art the anchor of the soul;
At Thy word the wind shall cease,
Storms be hushed to perfect peace.

Be Thou our haven of retreat,
A rock to fix our wavering feet;
Teach us to own Thy sovereign sway,
Whom the winds and seas obey.

Toplady, Augustus. *The Works of Augustus Toplady,*
London: J. Chidley. 1837, p. 888.

The Christian's Warfare

AUGUSTUS TOPLADY

Emptied of earth I fain would be,
The world, myself, and all but Thee;
Only reserved for Christ that died,
Surrendered to the crucified.

Sequestered from the noise and strife,
The lust, the pomp, and pride of life.

For heav'n alone my heart prepare,
And have my conversation there.

Oh, may I the Redeemer trace,
Invested with His righteousness!
This path, untired, I will pursue,
Nor slack while Jesus is in view.

Nothing save Jesus may I know,
My Father and companion Thou!
Lord, take my heart, assert my right,
And put all other loves to flight.

My idols tread beneath Thy feet,
And entered once, maintain Thy seat;
Let Dagon fall before Thy face,
The ark remaining in its place.

Oh, lend me now a two-edged sword,
To slay my sins before the Lord;
With Abraham's knife, before Thine eyes,
Each favorite Isaac sacrifice.

Toplady, Augustus. *The Works of Augustus Toplady, B.A.*
London: J. Chidley. 1837, p. 890.

Love to God

ISAAC WATTS

Happy the heart where graces reign,
Where love inspires the breast;
Love is the brightest of the train,
And strengthens all the rest.

Knowledge, alas, 'tis all in vain,
And all in vain our fear;
Our stubborn sins will fight and reign,
If love be absent there.

'Tis love that makes our cheerful feet
In swift obedience move;
The devils know and tremble too,
But Satan cannot love.

This is the grace that lives and sings
When faith and hope shall cease;
'Tis this shall strike our joyful strings
In the sweet realms of bliss.

Before we quite forsake our clay,
Or leave this dark abode,
The wings of love bear us away,
To see our smiling God.

Watts, Isaac. *The Psalms and Hymns of Isaac Watts.*
Morgan: Soli Deo Gloria Publications, 1997, pp. 428-429.

My Soul Follows Hard after Thee

JOHN MASON

My God, my God, my light, my love,
Mine all in all to me,
Wilt Thou a gracious Father prove
To souls that hang on Thee?

My God, my God, my light, my love,
For Thee I thirst alone;
The sweetest waters upon earth,
My soul accounts as none.

My God, my God, my light, my love,
Mine only, only Friend,
I seek, I long, I look for Thee,
Why wilt Thou not attend?

My God, my God, my light, my love,
Oh, wither art Thou gone?
Either be near unto me here,
Or lift me to Thy throne.

My God, my God, my light, my love,
Canst Thou that soul forsake,
That follows Thee with restless cries,
Longing to overtake?

My God, my God, my light, my love,
Thy child entreats Thy stay;
Father, shall not Thy bowels move?
Oh, turn and look this way.

My God, my God, my light, my love,
Come, come with me abide;
Delight me with Thy presence, Lord,
I know no joy beside.

My God, my God, my light, my love,
Hear Thou my mournful cry;
He hears, He hears me from above,
He will not see me die.

Mason, John. *Spiritual Songs, or Songs of Praise to Almighty God.*
Edinburgh: James Taylor, 1880, pp. 176-178.

Appeal to Christ for Sincerity of Love to Him

PHILIP DODDRIDGE

Do not I love Thee, O my Lord?
Behold my heart and see;
And turn each cursed idol out,
That dares to rival Thee.

Do not I love Thee from my soul?
Then let me nothing love;
Dead be my heart to every joy,
When Jesus cannot move.

Is not Thy name melodious still
To mine attentive ear;
Doth not each pulse with pleasure bound
My Savior's voice to hear?

Hast thou a lamb in all Thy flock,
I would disdain to feed?
Hast Thou a foe, before whose face
I fear Thy cause to plead?

Would not mine ardent spirit vie
With angels round the throne,
To execute Thy sacred will,
And make Thy glory known?

Would not my heart pour forth its blood
In honor of Thy name?
And challenge the cold hand of death
To damp the immortal flame.

Thou knowest I love Thee, dearest Lord;
But, oh, I long to soar
Far from the sphere of mortal joys,
And learn to love Thee more.

Doddridge, Philip. *The Miscellaneous Works of Philip Doddridge.*
London: Joseph Ogle Robinson, 1830, p. 1042.

To the Trinity

AUGUSTUS TOPLADY

Glorious union, God unsought;
Three in name and one in thought,
All Thy works Thy goodness show,
Center of perfection Thou!

Praise we, with uplifted eyes,
Him that dwells above the skies;
God who reigns on Zion's hill,
Made redeemed, and keeps us still.

Join the angelic hosts above,
Praise the Father's matchless love,
Who for us His Son hath given,
Sent Him to regain our heaven.

Glory to the Savior's grace,
Help of Adam's helpless race;
Who, for our transgressions slain,
Make us one with God again.

Next the Holy Ghost we bless;
He makes known and seals our peace,
Us he cleanses and makes whole,
Quickens every dying soul.

Holy, blessed, glorious Three,
One from all eternity,
Makes us vessels of Thy grace,
Ever running over with praise.

Thee we laud with grateful song,
Severed from the guilty throng,
Ransomed by the Son who died,
By the Spirit sanctified.

All the Persons join to raise
Sinners to a state of grace;
All united their bliss to ensure,
In the glorious work concur.

Oh, that we His love might taste;
Bless us, and we shall be blessed.
Cleanse us, Lord, from sin's abuse,
Fit us for the Master's use!

In our hearts, Thy temples dwell;
With the hope of glory fill.
Be on earth our Guest divine,
Then let heaven make us Thine.

Toplady, Augustus. *The Works of Augustus Toplady,*
London: J. Chidley. 1837, p. 895-896.

The Almighty Conqueror

·MATHER BYLES

Awake my heart, awake my tongue,
Sound each melodious string;
In numerous verse and lofty song,
To Thee, my God, I sing.

Omnipotent Redeemer-Lord,
What wonders hast Thou done!
My flowing numbers shall record,
The victories Thou has won.

I glow in raptures all divine,
As with the theme I rise;
Your tuneful aids, fictitious nine,
No more shall tempt my eyes.

Lo, robed with light, Jesus descends
The grave's tremendous gloom;
Day blushes round Him where He tends,
And dawns amid the tomb.

Sudden from off that dismal bed,
The scattering shadows fly;
The dark dominions of the dead
Confess the stranger, joy.

Hark, how in hideous howls complains,
The conquered tyrant death;
He roars aloud, and shakes his chains,
And grinds his iron teeth.

Immortal vigor filled the Man,
Almighty power the God,
When, armed with thunders, down He ran
To Satan's dire abode.

Then hell's grim monarch saw, and feared,
And felt his tottering throne;
He raged, and foamed, and wildly stared,
And seized his nodding crown.

In vain he raved, and rolled his eyes,
And held his crown in vain;
Swift on his head and lightning flies,
With everlasting pain.

At once the old serpent's craft was crushed,
Beneath the fiery frown,
When Thou, great God, resistless rushed,
And hurled the monster down.

The fetters, in the deep abyss,
His tortured members wring;
There let him writhe, and coil, and hiss,
And dart his pointless sting.

These were the victims of Thy hate,
When fury flushed Thy face;
But who, dear Savior, can relate
The conquest of Thy grace?

Cease, cease my tongue, be still, my lyre,
Be silent every string;
This is a theme, oh heavenly choir,
Too great for you to sing.

Byles, Mather. *Mather Byles' Works.*
Delmar: Scholars' Facsimiles & Reprints, 1978, pp. 1-4.

Knowledge and Affection

MEANS OF GRACE

Because knowledge and affection
Mutually help one another,
It is good to keep up our affections of love and delight
By all sweet inducements and divine encouragements,
For what the heart likes best, the mind studies most.
Those that can bring their hearts to delight in Christ
Know most of His ways.

— RICHARD SIBBES

Knowledge and Affection
MEANS OF GRACE

In the inward life, the heart reigns supreme. As the heart inwardly sees, tastes, and feels that which passes within, so it has the power to demand service and support for that which it relishes. As large as the world and universe are, they cannot satisfy the human heart, for it is still larger, and our hearts long to be filled. Only the Creator God, who made the human heart for His home, can fill our hearts to overflowing.

How shall Christians then get their wayward hearts, which are often filled with contrary desires, to delight in Christ? As Sibbes has indicated, by all sweet inducements and divine encouragements. While the author (root cause) of our delighting in Christ is God, He has ordained means by which we may inform our minds, thus keeping up our affections of love. One of the means of grace is reading Scripture—which is God's love letter to His people—memorizing it, studying it, hearing it preached, and meditating on it. Another means of grace is prayer—which is a time of conversing with our Redeemer—including personal, family, and corporate prayer. Other important means of grace observed corporately by the church are the sacraments of the Lord's Supper and Baptism.

The Puritans have said that it is the main purpose of the ministry to woo unto Christ, to display the loveliness of Christ, thus informing us of His desirability. Hearts that are prone to wander need the help of informed, transformed minds which have humbly availed themselves of the means of grace God has ordained for the good of His people. As we ask the Holy Spirit to alter the tastes of our souls, may we remember God has ordained means to accomplish the ends He desires.

The Means of Grace Which God Has Appointed

PHILIP DODDRIDGE

What kind provision God has made,
For this the prophets preached and wrote,
For this the blessed apostles taught;
Taught, as that Spirit did inspire,
Who fell from heaven in tongues of fire,
And gave them languages unknown,
That distant lands His grace might own.
His hand has kept the sacred page
Secure from men's and devils' rage.

For this, He churches did ordain,
His truths and worship to maintain;
For this, He pastors did provide,
In those assemblies to preside.
And from the round of common days
Marked out our sabbaths to His praise.
Delightful day, when Christians meet,
To hear, and pray, and sing—how sweet!

For this, He gives, in solemn ways,
Appointed tokens of His grace;
In sacramental pledges there,
His soldiers to their General swear.
Baptized into one common Lord,
They joyful meet around his board;
Honor the orders of His house,
And speak their love, and seal their vows.

Doddridge, Philip. *The Miscellaneous Works of Philip Doddridge.* London: Joseph Ogle Robinson, 1830, p. 1084.

The Altogether Lovely

MATHER BYLES

Oft has Thy name employed my muse,
Thou Lord of all above;
Oft has my song to Thee arose,
My song, inspired by love.

My heart has oft confessed in flame,
And melted all away;
Thou art by night my hourly dream,
My hourly thought by day.

Each feature o'er Thee is a charm,
And every limb a grace;
Divinely beauteous all Thy form,
Divinely fair Thy face.

Thy love to me how large, how full!
How kind are Thy commands!
Take, oh, my love, take all my soul,
Forever in Thy hands.

Those bleeding hands, which on the cross
Were stretched for my caress;
In the dear thought, my life I loose—
Was ever love like this!

Weep, weep my eyes, let gushing tears
Stream in an endless flow;
Love on His dying lips He wears,
His wounds compassion show.

Now He remembers me, and speaks,
I hear His voice, "Forgive";
In the dead pale that spreads His cheeks;
Ten thousand beauties live.

Lord, my affections all are Thine,
Warmed with a grateful fire;
And Thou, O best Beloved, art mine,
My hope, and my desire.

Conspiring love, conspiring charms,
Confess Thee all my joy;
Come, heavenly fair, come to my arms,
And all my powers employ.

Byles, Mather. *Mather Byles' Works.*
Delmar: Scholars' Facsimiles & Reprints, 1978, pp. 10-13.

The Heart Taken

JOHN NEWTON

The castle of the human heart,
Strong in its native sin,
Is guarded well in every part,
By him who dwells within.

For Satan there in arms resides,
And calls the place his own;
With care against assaults provides,
And rules as on a throne.

Each traitor thought, on him as chief,
In blind obedience waits;
And pride, self-will, and unbelief,
Are posted at the gates.

Thus Satan for a season reigns,
And keeps his goods in peace;
The soul is pleased to wear his chains,
Nor wishes a release.

But Jesus, stronger far than he,
In His appointed hour,
Appears to set His people free
From the usurper's power.

"This heart I bought with blood," He says,
"And now it shall be Mine."
His voice the strong one armed dismays,
He knows he must resign.

In spite of unbelief and pride,
And self and Satan's art,
The gates of brass fly open wide,
And Jesus wins the heart.

The rebel soul that once withstood
The Savior's kindest call,
Rejoices now, by grace subdued,
To serve Him with her all.

Newton, John. *The Works of the Rev. John Newton.*
Edinburgh: Thomas Nelson, 1841, p. 558.

The Assistance and Influence of the Blessed Spirit

PHILIP DODDRIDGE

'Tis not in my weak pow'r alone
To melt this stubborn heart of stone,
My soul to change, my life to mend,
Or seek to Christ, that gen'rous Friend.

'Tis God's own Spirit from above
Fixes our faith, inflames our love,
And makes a life divine begin
In wretched souls, long dead in sin.

That most important gift of heaven
To those that ask and seek is given;
Then be it my immediate care
With importunity of prayer,

To seek it in a Savior's name,
Who will not turn my hopes to shame.
God from on high, His grace shall pour,
My soul shall flourish more and more.

Press on with speed from grace to grace,
Till glory end and crown the race.
Since then the Father, and the Son,
And Holy Spirit, Three in one,

Glorious beyond all speech and thought,
Have jointly my salvation wrought;
I'll join them in my songs of praise,
Now and through heaven's eternal days.

Doddridge, Philip. *The Miscellaneous Works of Philip Doddridge.*
London: Joseph Ogle Robinson, 1830, p. 1084.

The Complaint and the Consolation

MATHER BYLES

Where shall I find my Lord, my love,
The Sovereign of my soul?
Pensive from east to west I rove,
And range from pole to pole.

I search the shady bowers, and trace
The mazes of the grove,
Dear Lord, to see Thy beauteous face,
And tell Thee how I love.

For Him, about the flow'ry fields,
My wandering footsteps stray,
When dewy morn each mountain guilds,
And purples o'er the sea;

Till evening bids the western clouds
With glittering edges flame,
To the soft winds, and murmuring floods,
I still repeat His name.

E'en in the silent shades of night,
My song the forest fills;
When the fair moon with solemn light
Has silvered o'er the hills,

"Jesus my fair," aloud I cry,
For Thee, for Thee I burn;
"Jesus," the echoing vales reply,
"Jesus," the rocks return.

Ah, Thou my life, when shall I taste,
That heaven of endless charms?
When shall I pant upon Thy breast,
And languish in Thy arms?

Oh, how I long to clasp Thee close,
Close in a strong caress!
Joyful my latest breath I'd loose
For so divine a bliss.

Ye lingering minutes, swiftly roll,
And rise, the happy day,
When on His bosom, thou my soul,
Shall all dissolve away.

Then shall my fluttering heart be fixed,
The muse no more complain;
But with the choirs immortal mixed,
Resound a heavenly strain.

Byles, Mather. *Mather Byles' Works.*
Delmar: Scholars' Facsimiles & Reprints, 1978, pp. 8-10.

The Lord Is My Portion

JOHN NEWTON

From pole to pole let others roam,
And search in vain for bliss;
My soul is satisfied at home,
The Lord my portion is.

Jesus, who on His glorious throne
Rules heav'n, and earth, and sea,
Is pleased to claim me for his own,
And give Himself to me.

His person fixes all my love,
His blood removes my fear;
And while He pleads for me above,
His arm preserves me here.

His word of promise is my food,
His Spirit is my guide;
Thus daily is my strength renewed,
And all my wants supplied.

For Him I count as gain each loss,
Disgrace, for Him, renown;
Well may I glory in my cross,
While He prepares my crown!

Let worldlings then indulge their boast,
How much they gain or spend;
Their joys must soon give up the ghost,
But mine shall know no end.

Newton, John. *The Works of the Rev. John Newton.*
Edinburgh: Thomas Nelson, 1841, p. 547.

Quick and Powerful Sword

THE WORD OF GOD

For the Word of God is living and powerful,
Sharper than any two-edged sword,
Piercing even to the division of soul and spirit,
and of joints and marrow,
And is a discerner of the thoughts and intents
of the heart.

— HEBREWS 4:12

Quick and Powerful Sword
THE WORD OF GOD

"Conversion turns us to the Word of God as our touchstone, to examine ourselves ... as our glass, to dress by (James 1), as our rule to walk and work by (Galatians 6:16), as our water to wash us (Psalm 119:9), as our fire to warm us (Luke 24), as our food to nourish us (Job 23:12), as our sword to fight with (Ephesians 6), as our counselor in all our doubts (Psalm 119:24), as our cordial to comfort us, and as our heritage to enrich us." (Henry, Philip. *A Puritan Golden Treasury.* Edinburgh: The Banner of Truth Trust, 1989, p. 33.)

Our hearts are often so cold and disaffected by the truths and realities of God. This world closes in upon us, chokes our desires, distracts our attention, and wears on our bodies. We need the quickening power of God and His Word to enable us to press on in the fight. The Word of God is a sword designed to be a discerner of the thoughts and intents of the heart, to which we need to apply ourselves when we are cold and weak. The Word needs to be read, studied, memorized, preached, and meditated upon.

"It is a great question for all ministers what it was that made that English minister [Charles Spurgeon] so living and so powerful himself, and so life-giving and so powerful to so many? You will remember what the play-actor said to the preacher who asked him why the theatre was so full while the church was so empty. 'Simply,' said the actor, 'because we act fiction as if it were fact; whereas you preach fact as if it were fiction.'" (Whyte, Alexander. *James Fraser Laird of Brea.* Edinburgh: Oliphant Anderson and Ferrier, 1889, p. 131.)

The Word–Quick and Powerful

JOHN NEWTON

The Word of Christ, our Lord,
With whom we have to do,
Is sharper than a two-edged sword,
To pierce the sinner through.

Swift as the lightning's blaze,
When awful thunders roll,
It fills the conscience with amaze,
And penetrates the soul.

No heart can be concealed
From His all-piercing eyes;
Each thought and purpose stands revealed,
Naked, without disguise.

He sees His people's fears,
He notes their mournful cry,
He counts their sighs and falling tears,
And helps them from on high.

Though feeble is their good,
It has its kind regard;
Yea, all they would do if they could,
Shall find a sure reward.

He sees the wicked too,
And will repay them soon,
For all the evil deeds they do,
And all they would have done.

Since all our secret ways
Are marked and known by Thee,
Afford us, Lord, Thy light of grace,
That we ourselves may see.

Newton, John. *The Works of the Rev. John Newton.*
Edinburgh: Thomas Nelson, 1841, p. 569.

The Holy Scriptures

ISAAC WATTS

Laden with guilt, and full of fears,
I fly to Thee, my Lord,
And not a glimpse of hope appears
But in Thy written Word.

The volume of my Father's grace
Does all my griefs assuage;
Here I behold my Savior's face,
Almost in every page.

This is the field where hidden lies
The pearl of price unknown;
That merchant is divinely wise
Who makes the pearl his own.

Here consecrated water flows,
To quench my thirst of sin;
Here the fair tree of knowledge grows,
Nor danger dwells therein.

This is the Judge that ends the strife,
Where wit and reason fail,
My guide to everlasting life,
Through all this gloomy vale.

Oh, may Thy counsels, mighty God,
My roving feet command;
Nor I forsake the happy road
That leads to Thy right hand.

Watts, Isaac. *The Psalms and Hymns of Isaac Watts.*
Morgan: Soli Deo Gloria Publications, 1997, p. 487.

The Riches of God's Word

SAMUEL STENNETT

Let avarice, from shore to shore,
Her favorite God pursue;
Thy Word, O Lord, we value more
Than India or Peru,

Here mines of knowledge, love, and joy,
Are opened to our sight;
The purest gold without alloy,
And gems divinely bright.

The councils of redeeming grace,
These sacred leaves unfold;
And here, the Savior's lovely face
Our raptured eyes behold.

Here, light descending from above
Directs our doubtful feet;
Here, promises of heavenly love,
Our ardent wishes meet.

Our numerous griefs are here redrest,
And all our wants supplied;
Nought we can ask to make us blessed
Is in this book denied.

For these inestimable gains,
That so enrich the mind,
Oh, may we search with eager pains,
Assured that we shall find!

Stennett, Samuel. *The Works of Samuel Stennett, D.D.*
London: Thomas Tegg, 1824, pp. 533-534.

The Light and Glory of the Word

JOHN NEWTON

The Spirit breathes upon the Word,
And brings the truth to sight;
Precepts and promises afford
A sanctifying light.

A glory gilds the sacred page,
Majestic like the sun;
It gives a light to every age,
It gives, but borrows none.

The hand that gave it still supplies
The gracious light and heat;
His truths upon the nations rise,
They rise, but never set.

Let everlasting thanks be Thine,
For such a bright display,
As makes a world of darkness shine
With beams of heavenly day,

My soul rejoices to pursue
The steps of Him I love;
Till glory breaks upon my view
In brighter worlds above.

Newton, John. *The Works of the Rev. John Newton.*
Edinburgh: Thomas Nelson, 1841, p. 591.

The Efficacy of God's Word

PHILIP DODDRIDGE

With reverend awe, tremendous Lord,
We hear the thunders of Thy Word.
The pride of Lebanon it breaks;
Swift the celestial fire descends,
The flinty rocks in pieces rends,
And earth to its deep center shakes.

Arrayed in majesty divine,
Here sanctity and justice shine,
And horror strikes the rebel through,
While loud this awful vice makes known
The wonders which Thy sword hath done,
And what Thy vengeance yet shall do.

So spread the honors of Thy name;
The terrors of a God proclaim;
Thick let the pointed arrows fly,
Till sinners, humbled in the dust,
Shall own the execution just,
And bless the hand by which they die.

Then clear the dark tempestuous day,
And radiant beams of love display;
Each prostrate soul let mercy raise;
So shall the bleeding captives feel,
Thy word, which gave the wound, can heal,
And change their groans to songs of praise.

Doddridge, Philip. *The Miscellaneous Works of Philip Doddridge.*
London: Joseph Ogle Robinson, 1830, pp. 1014-1015.

The Word More Precious Than Gold

JOHN NEWTON

Precious Bible—what a treasure
Does the Word of God afford!
All I want for life or pleasure,
Food and medicine, shield and sword;
Let the world account me poor,
Having this, I need no more.

Food to which the world's a stranger,
Here my hungry soul enjoys;
Of excess there is no danger,
Though it fills, it never cloys;
On a dying Christ I feed,
He is meat and drink indeed!

When my faith is faint and sickly,
Or when Satan wounds my mind,
Cordials to revive me quickly,
Healing medicines here I find;
To the promises I flee,
Each affords a remedy.

In the hour of dark temptation,
Satan cannot make me yield;
For the word of consolation,
Is to me a mighty shield;
While the Scripture truths are sure,
From his malice I'm secure.

Vain his threats to overcome me,
When I take the Spirit's sword;
Then, with ease, I drive him from me,
Satan trembles at the Word;
'Tis a sword for conquest made,
Keen the edge, and strong the blade.

Shall I envy, then, the miser,
Doting on his golden store?
Sure I am, or should be, wiser;
I am rich, 'tis he is poor;
Jesus gives me in His Word,
Food and medicine, shield and sword.

Newton, John. *The Works of the Rev. John Newton.*
Edinburgh: Thomas Nelson, 1841, p. 591.

Prayer for Ministers

JOHN NEWTON

Chief Shepherd of Thy chosen sheep,
From death and sin set free!
May every under-shepherd keep
His eye intent on Thee!

With plenteous grace their hearts prepare
To execute Thy will;
Compassion, patience, love, and care,
And faithfulness, and skill.

Inflame their minds with holy zeal,
Their flocks to feed and teach;
And let them live, and let them feel
The sacred truths they preach.

Oh, never let the sheep complain
That toys, which fools amuse,
Ambition, pleasure, praise, or gain,
Debase the shepherd's views.

The sword of God shall break his arm,
A blast shall blind his eye;
His word shall have no power to warm,
His gifts shall all grow dry.

"O Lord, avert this heavy woe,"
Let all Thy shepherds say;
And grace, and strength, on each bestow,
To labor while 'tis day.

He that for these forbears to feed
The souls whom Jesus loves,
Whatever he may profess or plead,
An idle shepherd proves.

Newton, John. *The Works of the Rev. John Newton.*
Edinburgh: Thomas Nelson, 1841, p. 587.

Ministers a Sweet Savor, Whether of Life or Death

PHILIP DODDRIDGE

Praise to the Lord on high, who spreads His triumph wide!
While Jesus' fragrant name is breathed on every side.
Balmy and rich, the odors rise,
And fill the earth, and reach the skies.

Ten thousand dying souls, its influence feel and live;
Sweeter than vital air, the incense they receive:
They breathe anew and rise and sing,
Jesus the Lord, their conquering King.

But sinners scorn the grace that brings salvation nigh;
They turn their face away, and faint, and fall, and die.
So sad a doom, ye saints, deplore,
For, oh, they fall, to rise no more.

Yet, wise and mighty God, shall all Thy servants be,
In those who live or die, a savor sweet to Thee;
Supremely bright, Thy grace shall shine,
Guarded with flames of wrath divine.

Doddridge, Philip. *The Miscellaneous Works of Philip Doddridge.*
London: Joseph Ogle Robinson, 1830, p. 273.

A Song of Praise for Gospel Ministry

JOHN MASON

Fair are the feet which bring the news of gladness unto me;
What happy messengers are these, which my blessed eyes do see!
These are the stars which God appoints for guides unto my way,
To lead me into Bethlehem-town, where my dear Savior lay.

These are my God's ambassadors, by whom His mind I know;
God's angels in His lower heaven, God's trumpeters below.
The trumpet sounds, the dead arise, which fell by Adam's hand;
Again the trumpet sounds, and they set forth for Canaan's land.

The servants speak, but Thou, Lord, dost a hearing ear bestow;
They smite the rock, but Thou, my God, dost make the waters flow.
They shoot the arrow, but Thy hand doth drive the arrow home;
They call, but, Lord, Thou dost compel and then Thy guests do come.

Angels that fly and worms that creep are both alike to Thee;
If Thou make worms Thine angels, Lord, they bring my God to me.
As sons of thunder first they come, and I the lightning fear;
But then they bring me to my home, and sons of comfort are.

Lord, Thou art in them of a truth, that I might never stray,
The clouds and pillars march before, and show me Canaan's way.
I bless my God, who is my Guide; I sing in Zion's ways;
When shall I sing on Zion's hill, Thine everlasting praise?

Mason, John. *Spiritual Songs, or Songs of Praise to Almighty God.*
Edinburgh: James Taylor, 1880, pp. 56-58.

A Prayer for Power on the Means of Grace

JOHN NEWTON

O Thou, at whose almighty Word
The glorious light from darkness sprung,
Thy quickening influence afford,
And clothe with power the preacher's tongue.

Though 'tis Thy truth he hopes to speak,
He cannot give the hearing ear;
'Tis Thine the stubborn heart to break,
And make the careless sinner fear.

As when of old the water flowed
Forth from the rock at Thy command,
Moses in vain had waved his rod,
Without Thy wonder-working hand.

As when the walls of Jericho,
Down to the earth at once were cast,
It was Thy power that brought them low,
And not the trumpet's feeble blast.

Thus we would in the means be found,
And thus on Thee alone depend,
To make the gospel's joyful sound
Effectual to the promised end.

Now, while we hear Thy Word of grace,
Let self and pride before it fall;
And rocky hearts dissolve apace,
In streams of sorrow at Thy call.

On all our youth assembled here,
The unction of Thy Spirit pour;
Nor let them lose another year,
Lest Thou shouldst strive and call no more.

Newton, John. *The Works of the Rev. John Newton.*
Edinburgh: Thomas Nelson, 1841, p. 577.

The Throne of Grace

PRAYER

Let us therefore come boldly to the throne of grace,
That we may obtain mercy
And find grace
To help in time of need.

— HEBREWS 4:16

The Throne of Grace
PRAYER

"I have known men who came to God for nothing else but just to come to Him, they so loved Him. They scorned to soil Him and themselves with any other errand than just purely to be alone with Him in His presence. Friendship is best kept up, even among men, by frequent visits; and the more free and frequent visits are, and the less occasioned by business, or necessity, or custom they are, the more friendly and welcome they are." (Thomas Goodwin, quoted in Whyte, Alexander. *The Spiritual Life: the Teaching of Thomas Goodwin.* Edinburgh; London: Oliphants Ltd., n.d., p. 23.)

It is said of Thomas Goodwin that he led a life captivated by prayer. Prayer was his refuge, his peace, his sanctification, his power. In fact, prayer became more a delight, and indeed, more an indulgence than a duty.

How do we approach prayer? Is it with a list of requests? Is it in a ritualistic pattern? Or is it an occasional panic stricken plea for help? We might rightly question the validity of a friendship in which our friend only came to us in such ways. Frequent visits with God just to enjoy being in His presence are few and far between in many schedules.

To delight in God's presence, indeed, to indulge ourselves by frequent unencumbered visits, is a depth in relationship few have known or tried. While God has extended an invitation to his children to come before his throne of grace at any time with our pleas and requests, let us also remember in His presence is fullness of joy. Go ahead, children of the living God, indulge yourselves!

The Throne of Grace

JOHN NEWTON

When Hannah, pressed with grief,
Poured forth her soul in prayer,
She quickly found relief,
And left her burden there.
Like her, in every trying case,
Let us approach the throne of grace.

When she began to pray,
Her heart was pained and sad;
But 'ere she went away,
Was comforted and glad.
In trouble what a resting-place
Have they who know the throne of grace.

Though men and devils rage,
And threaten to devour,
The saints, from age to age,
Are safe from all their power;
Fresh strength they gain to run their race,
By waiting at the throne of grace.

Eli her case mistook;
How was her spirit moved
By his unkind rebuke!
But God her cause approved.
We need not fear a creature's face,
While welcome at a throne of grace.

She was not filled with wine,
As Eli rashly thought;
But with a faith divine,
And found the help she sought.
Though men despise and call us base,
Still let us ply the throne of grace.

Men have not pow'r or skill
With troubled souls to hear;
Though they express goodwill,
Poor comforters they are.
But swelling sorrows sink apace,
When we approach the throne of grace.

Numbers before have tried,
And found the promise true;
Nor yet one been denied,
Then why should I or you?
Let us by faith their footsteps trace,
And hasten to the throne of grace.

As fogs obscure the light,
And taint the morning air,
But soon are put to flight,
If the bright sun appear.
Thus Jesus will our troubles chase,
By shining from the throne of grace.

Newton, John. *The Works of the Rev. John Newton.*
Edinburgh: Thomas Nelson, 1841, p. 533.

The Lord's Prayer

AUGUSTUS TOPLADY

Our holy Father, all Thy will
We fain would perfectly fulfill;
But each has left Thy law undone,
Unworthy to be called Thy son.

Who art in heaven, enthroned on high,
Diffusing glory through the sky;
Reigning above, on earth revered,
By saints beloved, by sinners feared.
Forever hallowed be Thy name,

The Triune God, the bright *I Am;*
At which seraphic choirs and all
The hosts of heav'n adoring fall.

Thy kingdom come; e'en now we wait
Thy glory to participate.
Rule in our hearts, unrivalled reign,
Nor e'er withdraw Thyself again.

Thy will, Thy law, Thy precept giv'n,
Be done on earth, as 'tis in heav'n;
Faithful as angels, fain would we
With covered faces wait on Thee.

Great God, on whom the ravens cry
For sustenance, our wants supply;
Give us this day, and evermore,
Our daily bread from hour to hour.

Forgive whatever we do amiss,
Our willful sins and trespasses,
As we forgive—reward us thus—
All them that trespass against us.

And lead us not by bounty's tide,
Into temptation, lust or pride;
But what by mercy we obtain,
Let power omnipotent restrain.

And, oh, deliver us Thine own
From evil and the evil one,
Who fain his darts in us would sheath,
And bind us with the chains of death.

Thou, Lord, canst vanquish his design,
Thine is the kingdom, only Thine;
The power, the eternal majesty,
And glory, appertain to Thee!

Toplady, Augustus. *The Works of Augustus Toplady.*
London: J. Chidley, 1837, p. 902.

Prayer

JOHN NEWTON

Behold the throne of grace!
The promise calls me near;
There Jesus shows a smiling face,
And waits to answer prayer.

That rich atoning blood,
Which sprinkled round I see,
Provides for those who come to God,
An all-prevailing plea.

My soul, ask what thou wilt,
Thou canst not be too bold;
Since His own blood for thee He spilled,
What else can He withhold?

Beyond thy utmost wants,
His love and power can bless;
To praying souls He always grants
More than they can express.

Since 'tis the Lord's command,
My mouth I open wide;
Lord, open Thou Thy bounteous hand,
That I may be supplied.

Thine image, Lord, bestow,
Thy presence and Thy love;
I ask to serve Thee here below,
And reign with Thee above.

Teach me to live by faith,
Conform my will to Thine;
Let me victorious be in death,
And then in glory shine.

If Thou these blessings give,
And wilt my portion be,
Cheerful the world's poor toys I leave
To them who know not Thee.

Newton, John. *The Works of the Rev. John Newton.*
Edinburgh: Thomas Nelson. 1841, p. 536.

God Invites Us to Come unto Him

JOHN NORDEN

Oh, what a joyful thing it is
To sing unto His praise,
Who lovingly embraceth His,
And guides them in His ways!

He calleth such as are oppressed,
And helps them by His might;
The poor oppressed gain them rest,
The wronged have their right.

Oh, come, therefore, and let us fall,
And humble us on knee
In hearty zeal; and then He shall
Of bondmen make us free.

His mercies, great and manifold,
Forthwith He will extend;
His favors far surpass the gold,
Whose glory shall have end.

Let us therefore sing out in zeal,
That people all may know,
That He to His doth still reveal
His secrets here below.

His heavenly heart's ease they shall find,
Who do perform His will;
But worldly men continue blind,
Vainly conceited still.

Oh, teach us, Lord, teach us in love,
What we should do and say;
Give us directions from above,
How we may rightly pray.

That we to Thee may honor give,
And to our children show,
How Thou Thy servants dost relieve
That want Thine aid below.

Norden, John. *A Progress of Piety.*
Cambridge: University Press, 1968, pp. 32-33 ("God Accepts Us to Come to Him").

Ask What I Shall Give Thee

JOHN NEWTON

Come, my soul, thy suit prepare,
Jesus loves to answer prayer;
He Himself has bid thee pray,
Therefore will not say thee nay.

Thou art coming to a King,
Large petitions with thee bring;
For His grace and power are such,
None can ever ask too much.

With my burden I begin,
Lord, remove this load of sin!
Let Thy blood, for sinners spilled,
Set my conscience free from guilt.

Lord, I come to Thee for rest,
Take possession of my breast;
There Thy blood-bought right maintain,
And without a rival reign.

As the image in the glass
Answers the beholder's face;
Thus unto my heart appear,
Print Thine own resemblance there.

While I am a pilgrim here,
Let Thy love my spirit cheer;
As my Guide, my Guard, my Friend,
Lead me to my journey's end.

Show me what I have to do,
Every hour my strength renew;
Let me live a life of faith,
Let me die Thy people's death.

Newton, John. *The Works of the Rev. John Newton.*
Edinburgh: Thomas Nelson. 1841, p. 535.

A Song of Praise for Answer to Prayer

JOHN MASON

What are the heavens, O God of heaven?
Thou art more bright, more high?
What are bright stars, and brighter saints
To Thy bright majesty?
Thou art far above the songs of heaven,
Sung by the holy ones;
And dost Thou stoop, and bow Thine ear,
To a poor sinner's groans?

God minds the language of my heart,
My groans and sighs He hears;
He hath a book for my requests,
A bottle for my tears.
But did not my Savior's blood
First wash away my guilt,
My sighs would prove but empty air,
My tears would all be spilt.

Lord, Thine eternal Spirit was
My Advocate within;
But, oh, my smoke joined with Thy flame,
My prayer was mixed with sin.
But then Christ was my Altar, and
My Advocate above;
His blood did clear my prayer, and gained
An answer full of love.

It could not be that Thou shouldst hear
A mortal, sinful worm;
But that my prayers presented are
In a more glorious form.
Christ's precious hands took my requests,
And turned my dross to gold;
His blood put warmth into my prayers,
Which were by nature cold.

Thou heardst my groans for Jesus' sake,
Whom Thou dost hear always;
Lord, hear through that prevailing name,
My voice of joy and praise.

Mason, John. *Spiritual Songs, or Songs of Praise to Almighty God.*
Edinburgh: James Taylor, 1880, pp. 80-82.

Visible Sermons

SACRAMENTS

A sacrament is a visible sermon.
And herein the sacrament excels the Word preached.
The Word is a trumpet to proclaim Christ;
The sacrament is a glass to represent Him.

— THOMAS WATSON

Visible Sermons
SACRAMENTS

God designed the sacraments to remind His covenant people of the washing away of their sin and their being clothed with Christ's righteousness. Since they are united with Christ and each other, they dine at His table, where they are spiritually nourished and fed by Christ Himself. Thankfully they muse upon the benefits He purchased for them, as they look with longing eyes for their Savior's return.

God's love, mercy, and grace are on display in these visual sermons. However, God's grace is seen as adding even more brilliance to mercy and love for its condescension—its downward flow. Love may take different directions. There is the upward direction of love where a person may show love to one who holds a position of authority over them. There is the downward direction of love as a parent loves a child. Yet, though a subject may love his king and be devoted to him, we do not hear of a subject extending grace to his king, nor a child to his parent. Grace has but one direction—it always flows downward. God's grace is extended to undeserving sinners who have merited nothing but damnation. Redeemed sinners should be ever rejoicing in the overpowering, downward flow of grace which sweeps over them and bathes them in Christ's cleansing blood.

As God's children participate in the sacraments, may the beautiful mirrored image of their Savior cause their souls to wonder anew at the downward flow of God's grace.

The Design and Obligation of Baptism

PHILIP DODDRIDGE

In baptism washed we all must be,
In honor of the sacred Three;
To show how we are washed from sin,
In Jesus' blood, and born again,

By grace divine; and thus are made
Members of Christ our common Head.
The Father formed the glorious scheme,
And we adopted are by Him.

The Son, great Prophet, Priest, and King,
Did news of this redemption bring;
He by His death our life procured,
And now bestows it as our Lord.

The Holy Spirit witness bore
To this blessed gospel heretofore;
And teaches those He's purified,
Faithful and patient to abide.

Into these names was I baptized;
And be the honor justly prized.
Nor let the sacred bond be broke,
Nor be my covenant God forsook.

Thus washed I'd keep my garments clean,
And never more return to sin.
One body now all Christians are;
Oh, may they in one Spirit share!
And cherish that endearing love,
In which the saints are blessed above!

Doddridge, Philip. *The Miscellaneous Works of Philip Doddridge.*
London: Joseph Ogle Robinson, 1830, pp. 1084-1085.

A Song of Praise for Holy Baptism

JOHN MASON

Lord, what is man, that lump of sin,
Made up of earth and hell,
Not fit to come within the camp,
Where holy angels dwell?
Man is a leper from the womb,
An Ethiopian born,
A traitor's guilty son and heir,
Worthy of pain and scorn.

And dost Thou look on such a one?
Are not Thine eyes most pure?
But they are eyes of pity too,
Where griefs do beg a cure.
This leper is a loathsome sight,
But pity casts an eye,
And bids him wash in Jordan's streams,
To cure his leprosy.

This Ethiopian skin is changed,
And made as white as snow,
When dipped in wonder-working streams
Which from Christ's side did flow.
As Adam slept, and from his side,
A killing Eve arose;
From my pierced Lord, that smitten Rock,
A pure life-fountain flows.

Ah, what a tainted wretch is man;
And so he must have stood.
But lo, an act of sovereign grace
Restores him to His blood.
Save me, my God, for I am Thine;
Lord, own Thy seal to me;
Oh, wash my soul, till it be cleansed,
And purified for Thee.

Blessed above streams is Jordan's flood,
Which toucheth Canaan's shore;
I'll sing Thy praise in Jordan's streams,
In Canaan evermore.

Mason, John. *Spiritual Songs, or Songs of Praise to Almighty God.*
Edinburgh: James Taylor, 1880, pp. 58-60.

Before the Sacrament of the Lord's Supper
WILLIAM BURKITT

This day the Lord of Hosts invites
Unto a costly feast;
I will take care, and will prepare
To be a welcome guest.

But who and what am I, O Lord!
Unholy and unfit
To come within Thy doors, or at
Thy table for to sit.

Awake repentance, faith, and love;
Awake, oh, every grace;
To meet your Lord with one accord,
In His most holy place.

Worldly distraction stay behind,
Below the mount abide;
Cause no disturbance in my mind,
To make my Savior chide.

Oh, come, my Lord, the time draws nigh,
That I am to receive;
Stand with my pardon sealed by
Persuade me to believe.

Let not my Jesus now be strange,
Nor hide Himself from me,
But cause Thy face to shine upon
The soul that longs for Thee.

Come, blessed Spirit, from above!
My soul do Thou inspire
To approach the table of the Lord
With fullness of desire.

Oh, let our entertainment now
Be so exceeding sweet,
That we may long to come again,
And at Thy altar meet.

Burkitt, William. *A Help and Guide to Christian Families.*
London: Longman, Hurst, and Co. and J. Mawman, 1822, pp. 144-145.

Welcome to the Table

JOHN NEWTON

This is the feast of heavenly wine,
And God invites to sup;
The juices of the living vine
Were pressed, to fill the cup.

Oh, bless the Savior, ye that eat,
With royal dainties fed;
Not heaven affords a costlier treat,
For Jesus is the bread.

The vile, the lost, He calls to them,
Ye trembling souls, appear!
The righteous in their own esteem
Have no acceptance here.

Approach, ye poor, nor dare refuse
The banquet spread for you;
Dear Savior, this is welcome news,
Then I may venture too.

If guilt and sin afford a plea,
And may obtain a place,
Surely the Lord will welcome me,
And I shall see His face.

Newton, John. *The Works of the Rev. John Newton.*
Edinburgh: Thomas Nelson, 1841, p. 588.

Christ Present in Faith Upon the Gospel Table

RALPH ERSKINE

Jesus is gone above the skies,
Where now we see Him not;
And carnal objects court our eyes,
To thrust Him from our thought.

He knows what wandering hearts we have,
Forgetful of His face;
And, to refresh our minds, He gave
Memorials of His grace.

He oft the gospel-table spreads
With His own flesh and blood;
Faith on the rich provision feeds,
And tastes the love of God.

While He is absent from our sight,
'Tis to prepare a place,
Where we may dwell in heavenly light,
Forever near His face.

Erskine, Ralph. *Erskine's Sermons and Practical Works.*
Aberdeen: A. King & Co., 1863, VII:603.

Communion with Christ and with the Saints

ISAAC WATTS

Jesus invites His saints
To meet around His board;
Here pardoned rebels sit and hold
Communion with their Lord.

For food He gives His flesh,
He bids us drink His blood;
Amazing favor, matchless grace
Of our descending God!

This holy bread and wine
Maintains our fainting breath,
By union with our living Lord,
And interest in His death.

Our heavenly Father calls
Christ and His members one;
We, the young children of His love,
And He, the firstborn Son.

We are but several parts
Of the same broken bread;
One body hath its several limbs,
But Jesus is the Head.

Let all our powers be joined
His glorious name to raise;
Pleasure and love fill every mind,
And every voice be praise.

Watts, Isaac. *The Psalms and Hymns of Isaac Watts.*
Morgan: Soli Deo Gloria Publications, 1997, p. 523.

Christ Crucified

JOHN NEWTON

When on the cross my Lord I see,
Bleeding to death for wretched me,
Satan and sin no more can move,
For I am all transformed to love.

His thorns and nails pierce through my heart,
In every groan I bear a part;
I view His wounds with streaming eyes;
But see, He bows His head, and dies.

Come sinners, view the Lamb of God,
Wounded, and dead, and bathed in blood;
Behold His side, and venture near,
The well of endless life is here.

Here I forget my cares and pains;
I drink, yet still my thirst remains;
Only the fountainhead above
Can satisfy the thirst of love.

Oh, that I thus could always feel;
Lord, more and more Thy love reveal.
Then my glad tongue shall loud proclaim
The grace and glory of Thy name.

Thy name dispels my guilt and fear,
Revives my heart and charms my ear;
Affords a balm for every wound,
And Satan trembles at the sound.

Newton, John. *The Works of the Rev. John Newton.*
Edinburgh: Thomas Nelson, 1841, p. 589.

The Experience

EDWARD TAYLOR

Oh, that I always breathed in such an air,
As I sucked in, feeding on sweet content;
Dished up unto my soul even in that prayer,
Poured out to God over last sacrament.
What beam of light wrapped up my sight to find
Me nearer God than 'ere came in my mind?

Most strange it was; but yet more strange that shine,
Which filled my soul then to the brim to spy
My nature with Thy nature all divine,
Together joined in Him—that's Thou, and I.
Flesh of my flesh, bone of my bone. There's run
Thy Godhead, and my manhood in Thy Son.

Oh, that flame which Thou didst on me cast,
Might me inflame, and lighten everywhere.
Then heaven to me would be less at last,
So much of heaven I should have while here.
Oh, sweet though short, I'll not forget the same;
My nearness, Lord, to Thee did me inflame.

I'll claim my right; give place, ye angels bright.
Ye further from the Godhead stand than I.
My nature is your Lord; and doth unite
Better than yours unto the Deity.
God's throne is first and mine is next; to you
Only the place of waiting men is due.

Oh, that my heart, Thy golden harp might be
Well tuned by glorious grace, that every string,
Screwed to the highest pitch, might unto Thee
All praises wrapped in sweetest music bring.
I praise Thee, Lord, and better praise Thee would
If what I had, my heart might ever hold.

Taylor, Edward. *Early New England Meditative Poetry.*
New York: Paulist Press, 1988, p. 162.

My Flesh Is Meat Indeed

SAMUEL STENNETT

Here at Thy table, Lord, we meet
To feed on food divine;
Thy body is the bread we eat,
Thy precious blood the wine.

He that prepares the rich repast,
Himself comes down and dies;
And He invites us thus to feast
Upon the sacrifice.

The bitter torments he endured
Upon the shameful cross,
For us, His welcome guests, procured
These heart-reviving joys.

His body torn with rudest hands
Becomes the finest bread;
And with the blessing He commands,
Our noblest hopes are fed.

His blood, that from each opening vein,
In purple torrents ran,
Hath filled this cup with generous wine,
That cheers both God and man.

Sure there was never love so free,
Dear Savior, so divine!
Well Thou may claim that heart of me,
Which owes so much to Thine.

Yes, Thou shalt surely have my heart,
My soul, my strength, my all;
With life itself I'll freely part,
My Jesus, at Thy call.

Stennett, Samuel. *The Works of Samuel Stennett, D.D.*
London: Thomas Tegg, 1824, p. 550.

A Song of Praise for the Lord's Supper

JOHN MASON

Oh, praise the Lord, praise Him, praise Him,
Sing praises to His name;
O all ye saints of heaven and earth,
Extol and laud the same;
Who spared not His only Son,
But gave Him for us all,
And made Him drink the cup of wrath,
The wormwood and the gall.

Frail nature shrunk, and did request
That bitter cup might pass;
But He must drink it off, and this
The Father's pleasure was.
"Lo then I come to do Thy will,"
His blessed Son replied;
Yielding Himself to God and man
He stretched His arms and died.

He died indeed, but rose again,
And did ascend on high,
That we poor sinners, lost and dead,
Might live eternally.
Good Lord, how many souls in hell
Doth vengeance vex and fear?
Were it not for a dying Christ,
Our dwelling had been there.

His blood was shed instead of ours,
His soul our hell did bear;
He took our sin, gave us Himself,
What an exchange is here!

Whatever is not hell itself,
For me it is too good:
But must we eat the flesh of Christ?
And must we drink His blood?

His flesh is heavenly food indeed,
His blood is drink divine;
His graces drop as honey-falls,
His comforts taste like wine.
Sweet Christ, Thou hast refreshed our souls
With Thine abundant grace;
For which we magnify Thy name,
Longing to see Thy face.

When shall our souls mount up to Thee,
Most holy, just and true,
To eat that bread, and drink that wine,
Which is forever new?

Mason, John. *Spiritual Songs, or Songs of Praise to Almighty God.*
Edinburgh: James Taylor, 1880, pp. 60-62.

After the Sacrament of the Lord's Supper

WILLIAM BURKITT

Lord, any mercy short of hell,
For me it is too good;
But have I eaten the flesh of Christ,
And also drank His blood?

Mysterious depths of endless love
My admiration raise!
O God, Thy name exalted is
Above the highest praise!

My Savior's flesh is meat indeed,
His blood is drink divine;
His graces drop like honeycombs,
His comforts taste like wine.

This day has Christ refreshed my soul
With His abundant grace;
For which I magnify His name,
Longing to see His face.

When shall my soul ascend on high,
Most holy, just, and true,
To eat that bread and drink that wine
Which is forever new?

To Him that sits upon the throne,
The Lamb whom we adore,
Be glory, blessing, strength, renown,
And honor evermore.

Burkitt, William. *An Help and Guide to Christian Families.*
London: Longman, Hurst, and Co. and J. Mawman, 1822, pp. 145-146.

Hearts
Kept in Tune

SELF-EXAMINATION

Keep your heart with all diligence,
For out of it spring the issues of life.
— PROVERBS 4:23

Hearts Kept in Tune
SELF-EXAMINATION

"For though grace has, in a great measure, rectified the soul and given it a habitual and heavenly temper, yet sin often actually discomposes it again. Thus even a gracious heart is like a musical instrument which, though it is never so exactly tuned, a small matter brings out of tune again. Yes, hang it aside but a little and it will need tuning again before you can play another lesson on it. Even so stands the case with gracious hearts." (Flavel, John. *Keeping the Heart.* Morgan, Pa: Soli Deo Gloria, 1998, p. 6.)

Though God has graciously given us, through Christ, a new heart with "a habitual and heavenly temper," let us not forget that our hearts have not yet been completely made perfect. Often the love song we desire to play for our Savior is not a sweet, melodious sonnet, for the sin around us and, indeed, in us causes it to be off key. Often we even fail to realize how bad we sound for many of the songs around us are hopelessly out of tune also.

This is why we need to step aside by ourselves for a quiet reflective time of tuning (self-examination). Using God's Word as our pitch fork, out of tune souls will be set again. Strings that have become loose (by neglect of Bible reading and prayer) need to be tightened. As conscientious musicians, we will avoid sinful circumstances that we know will cause our hearts to sound a sourer note.

Fellow Christians, before we play another melody, let us ask God to train our ears to hear and to delight in His song—His will and His ways. And by the Holy Spirit enabling, may this orchestra of redeemed sinners play a fine tuned cantata with the sweet notes of holiness for the world and our Savior to hear.

For the Morning

AUGUSTUS TOPLADY

My soul, canst thou no higher rise,
To meet thy God, than this?
Yet, Lord, accept my sacrifice,
Defective as it is.

Tune all my organs to Thy praise,
And psalmist's muse impart;
And, with thy penetrating rays,
Oh, melt my frozen heart.

Give me Thyself, the only good,
And ever with me stay;
Whose faithful mercies are renewed
With each returning day.

Ah, guide me with a Father's eye,
Nor from my soul depart;
But let the Daystar from on high
Illuminate my heart.

This day preserve me without sin,
Unspotted in Thy ways;
And hear me while I usher in
The welcome dawn with praise.

Far as the east from west remove
Each earthly vain desire,
And raise me on the wings of love,
Till I can mount no higher.

Toplady, Augustus. *The Works of Augustus Toplady.*
London: J. Chidley, 1837, p. 891.

The Excellence of Peace of Conscience

BENJAMIN KEACH

My conscience is become my friend,
And cheerfully doth speak to me;
And I will to his motions bend,
Though that I should reproached be;
I matter not who doth revile,
Since conscience in my face doth smile.

My conscience now doth give me rest,
My burdens gone, my soul is free;
Again I would not be oppressed,
In the old bands of misery.
For kingdoms, nor for crowns of gold,
Nor anything that can be sold.

My conscience doth with precious food,
Keep my poor soul continually;
It dainties also that are good,
All sinful sweets I do defy,
This banquet's lasting, 'twill supply
My wants and me until I die.

My conscience doth me cheerful make,
When I am much possessed with grief,
And when I suffer for it's sake,
'Twill yield me joy and sweet relief;
Though troubles rise and much increase,
I, in my conscience, shall have peace.

When others to the mountains fly,
And some amazed do trembling stand,
A place of shelter there have I,
And conscience will lend me his hand,
To lock me in his chambers fast,
Until the indignation's past.

At death, and in the judgment day,
What would men give for such a friend!
All those which do him disobey,
They will repent, I'm sure, in the end.
When such are forced to howl and cry,
My soul shall sing eternally.

Keach, Benjamin. *War with the Devil.*
London: E. Johnston, 1771, pp. 90-91.

The Contrite Heart

JOHN NEWTON

The Lord will happiness divine,
On contrite hearts bestow;
Then tell me, gracious God, is mine,
A contrite heart or no?

I hear, but seem to hear in vain,
Insensible as steel;
If ought is felt, 'tis only pain,
To find I cannot feel.

I sometimes think myself inclined
To love Thee if I could,
But often feel another mind,
Averse to all that's good

My best desires are faint and few,
I fain would strive for more;
But when I cry, "My strength renew,"
Seem weaker than before.

Thy saints are comfortable, I know,
And love Thy house of prayer;
I therefore go where others go,
But find no comfort there.

Newton, John. *The Works of the Rev. John Newton.*
Edinburgh: Thomas Nelson, 1841, p. 546.

Spiritual Inactivity Lamented

SAMUEL DAVIES

Jesus, what eager zeal inspired
Thy heart to die for me?
Oh, that my languid breast were fired
With equal flame to Thee!

But how has sin benumbed my soul,
My heart how hard and dead;
My softest passions, ah how dull,
Heavy and cold as lead.

Meantime inferior toys can charm,
And all my passions move;
A friend or relative can warm,
And melt my heart to love.

My thoughts refuse to soar to Thee,
But full of vigor spring
To chase some gilded vanity,
Some useless, trifling thing.

Blessed Jesus, I would rather lose
My thinking faculty,
Than waste my thoughts on trifles thus,
And never think of Thee.
If my soft passions be not Thine,
My passions are a pain;
Let me the power of love resign,
Rather than love in vain.

Lord, 'tis a curse to live and breathe,
Unless I live to Thee;
If I must lie thus stupid, death
Is better than to be.

Thy quickening energy exert,
Blessed Jesus, and bestow
A living soul, a tender heart
To serve my God below.

Davies, Samuel. *Collected Poems of Samuel Davies.*
Gainsville: Scholars' Facsimiles & Reprints, 1968, pp. 108-109.

For a Soft Heart

JOHN MASON

That heart is harder than a stone,
That rises up to play;
And never with sorrow thinks upon
The sins of yesterday.
The last night's failures well might make,
If they were duly scanned,
Each rock, each sinner's heart to ache,
For saints are daily tanned.

Ah, Lord, dost Thou not see my heart?
Alas, how little love!
I pray Thee, do not lose Thy part;
Drop softness from above.
Oh, keep it tender, keep it soft,
That I may know to raise,
And quickly fit the lowest string,
Unto a tune of praise.

Thy people do lament and cry,
Their sins have made them groan;
Give me their frames, then so shall I,
Lord, roll away this stone.
If Thou withhold a little space,
Withhold not very long;
Send down the melting dews of grace,
I'll send Thee up a song.

Make my heart softer, softer still,
Me like Thy mourning dove;
I mourn because I cannot mourn,
But, Lord, Thou knowest I love.
Make my heart softer, softer still,
That, by Thy gracious hand.
A deep impression may be made
Even from the least command.

Mason, John. *Spiritual Songs, or Songs of Praise to Almighty God.* Edinburgh: James Taylor, 1880, pp. 153-155.

For All the Mind of Christ

AUGUSTUS TOPLADY

Hail, faultless Model, sinless Guide,
In whom no blame was seen;
Able Thou wert, and none beside,
To ransom guilty men.

I want my happiness below,
In Thee alone to find;
Surely Thou wilt on me bestow
Thy pure, Thy heavenly mind!

Active for God, I fain would be,
And do my work assigned;
Jesus, look down, implant in me,
Thy zealous fervent mind!

While here, it was Thy constant aim
To benefit mankind.
Oh, give me, dear redeeming Lamb,
Thy loving, gracious mind!

Stiff is my neck, and proud my heart,
Unbroken, unresigned;
When wilt Thou, blessed Lord, impart
Thy patient, humble mind?

My sins how slowly do I leave,
To earthly things inclined;
But wean me, Lord, and let me have
Thy self-denying mind.

Oh, might I walk with faithful heed,
And look no more behind,
Possessed of what I chiefly need,
Thy serious steady mind.

Still may my every grace increase,
Till I in heaven appear;
On earth like Thee in holiness,
Like Thee in glory there.

Toplady, Augustus. *The Works of Augustus Toplady.*
London: J. Chidley, 1837, p. 894.

The Holy Spirit Invoked

SAMUEL DAVIES

Eternal Spirit, source of light,
Enliv'ning, consecrating fire,
Descend, and with celestial heat,
Our dull, our frozen hearts inspire;
Our souls refine, our dross consume.
Come, condescending Spirit, come!

In our cold breasts, oh, strike a spark
Of the pure flame which seraphs feel,
Nor let us wander in the dark,
Or lie benumbed and stupid still.
Come, vivifying Spirit, come,
And make our hearts Thy constant home.

Whatever guilt and madness dare,
We would not quench the heav'nly fire;
Our hearts as fuel we prepare,
Though in the flame we should expire.
Our breasts expand to make Thee room;
Come, purifying Spirit, come!

Let pure devotion's fervors rise;
Let every pious passion glow.
Oh, let the raptures of the skies,
Kindle in our cold hearts below.
Come, condescending Spirit, come,
And make our souls Thy constant home!

Davies, Samuel. *Collected Poems of Samuel Davies.*
Gainsville: Scholars' Facsimiles & Reprints, 1968, pp. 189-190.

Searching and Trying Our Ways

PHILIP DODDRIDGE

Thy piercing eye, O God, surveys
The various windings of our ways;
Teach us their tendency to know,
And judge the paths in which we go.

How wild, how crooked have they been,
A maze of foolishness and sin!
With all the light we vainly boast,
Leaving our guide, our souls are lost.

Had not Thy mercy been our aid,
So fatally our feet had strayed;
Stern justice had its prisoners led
Down to the chambers of the dead.

Oh, turn us back to Thee again,
Or we shall search our ways in vain;
Shine, and the path of life reveal,
And bear us on to Zion's hill.

Roll on, ye swift revolving years,
And end this round of sins and cares;
No more a wanderer would I roam,
But near my Father fix a home.

Doddridge, Philip. *The Miscellaneous Works of Philip Doddridge.*
London: Joseph Robinson, 1830, p. 1016.

The Inconsistencies of Our Love

ISAAC WATTS

Why is my heart so far from Thee,
My God, my chief delight?
Why are my thoughts no more by day
With Thee, no more by night?

Why should my foolish passions rove?
Where can such sweetness be,
As I have tasted in Thy love,
As I have found in Thee?

When my forgetful soul renews
The savor of Thy grace,
My heart presumes I cannot lose
The relish all my days.

But 'ere one fleeting hour is passed,
The flattering world employs
Some sensual bait to seize my taste,
And to pollute my joys.

Trifles of nature or of art,
With fair, deceitful charms,
Intrude into my thoughtless heart,
And thrust me from Thy arms.

Then I repent, and vex my soul,
That I should leave Thee so;
Where will those wild affections roll
That let a Savior go?

Sin's promised joys are turned to pain,
And I am drowned in grief;
But my dear Lord returns again,
He flies to my relief.

Seizing my soul with sweet surprise,
He draws with loving bands;
Divine compassion in His eyes,
And pardon in His hands.

Wretch that I am, to wander thus
In chase of false delight;
Let me be fastened to Thy cross,
Rather than lose Thy sight.

Make haste, my days, to reach the goal,
And bring my heart to rest,
On the dear center of my soul,
My God, my Savior's breast.

Watts, Isaac. *The Psalms and Hymns of Isaac Watts.*
Morgan: Soli Deo Gloria Publications, 1997, pp. 415-416.

Mysteries about the Saint's Work and Warfare:

Sins, Sorrows and Joys

RALPH ERSKINE

The work is great I'm called unto,
Yet nothing's left for me to do;
Hence for my work heav'n has prepared
No wages, yet a great reward.

To works, but not to working dead;
From sin, but not from sinning freed.
I clear myself from no offence,
Yet wash my hands in innocence.

My Father's anger burns like fire,
Without a spark of furious ire;
Though still my sins displeasing be,
Yet still I know He's pleased with me.

Triumphing is my constant trade,
Who yet am often captive led;
My bloody war does never cease,
Yet I maintain a stable peace.

My foes assaulting conquer me,
Yet never obtain the victory;
For all my battles lost or won,
Were gained before they were begun.

I'm still at ease, and still oppressed;
Have constant trouble, constant rest;
Both clear and cloudy, free and bound;
Both dead and living, lost and found.

Sin for my good does work and win;
Yet 'tis not good for me to sin.
My pleasure issues from my pain;
My losses still increase my gain.

I'm healed even when my plagues abound,
Covered with dust even when I'm crowned;
As low as death, when living high;
Nor shall I live, yet cannot die.

For all my sins my heart is sad,
Since God's dishonored; yet I'm glad,
Though once I was a slave to sin,
Since God does thereby honor win.

My sins are ever in His eye,
Yet He beholds no sin in me,
His mind that keeps them all in store,
Will yet remember them no more.

Because my sins are great, I feel
Great fears of heavy wrath; yet still
For mercy seek, for pardon wait,
Because my sins are very great.

I hope when plunged into despair,
I tremble when I have no fear.
Pardons dispel my griefs and fears,
And yet dissolve my heart in tears.

Erskine, Ralph. *Erskine's Sermons and Practical Works.*
Aberdeen: A. King & Co., 1863, VII:177-178.

Love to God for His Holiness

SAMUEL DAVIES

Come, Holy Spirit, come inflame
Our lukewarm hearts with sacred fire;
May all our passions, to Thy name,
In transports most refined, aspire.

May love sublime our hearts possess,
From every selfish mixture free,
Fired with charms of holiness,
The beauty of divinity.

We see the beauty of Thy grace,
That saves rebellious worms from hell;
But ah, the charms of holiness,
We dimly see, and faintly feel.

Selfish and mercenary views
Are with our purest passions mixed;
A nobler passion, oh, infuse,
On holiness supremely fixed.

Thus in the glorious worlds on high,
Where holiness is most adored,
The angelic choirs incessant cry,
"Thrice holy, holy, holy Lord!"

Refine our hearts, inspire our tongue,
And we in humble notes below,
Will imitate the heavenly song,
And echo, "Holy, holy," too.

Davies, Samuel. *Collected Poems of Samuel Davies.*
Gainsville: Scholars' Facsimiles & Reprints, 1968, pp. 100-101.

Stooping Down Low

PRIDE AND HUMILITY

All virtue is founded in truth;
And so our humility is founded in a true and just sense
Of our weakness, misery, and sin.
He who rightly sees and feels his sinful condition
Will always live in humility.

— WILLIAM LAW

Stooping Down Low
PRIDE AND HUMILITY

Scottish theologian and pastor Samuel Rutherford counseled his parishioner John Gordon: "Dear Sir, I always saw nature mighty, lofty, heady, and strong in you; and that it was more for you to be mortified and dead to the world, than for another common man. Ye will take a low ebb, and a deep cut, and a long lance, to go to the bottom of your wounds in saving humiliation, to make you a won prey for Christ. Be humble; walk softly. Down, down, for God's sake, my dear and worthy brother, with your topsail. Stoop, Stoop! It is a low entry to go in at heaven's gate." (Rutherford, Samuel. *The Letters of Samuel Rutherford.* Edinburgh: The Banner of Truth Trust, 1984, p. 172.)

It is indeed a low entry to admit that, in and of ourselves, we have no righteousness, but we must seek our righteousness at the hands of Another (Jesus). Many try to lessen the stoop in entering heaven by arguing on their own reduced and easier terms of salvation, only to have their heads knocked off upon entrance. It is not an easy task to admit that all we do—in our prayers, in our various ministries, in our giving, even in our quiet times—have mixed motives, mixed affections, and mixed aims. Yes, all are tainted with sin. These supposed righteous deeds are much less than the perfection which is God's standard of righteousness. Stoop, stoop, for this is a very low entry to go in at heaven's gate.

There is no room for pride or boasting when we rightly see and feel our sinful condition. A believer who is grounded in truth will cling to Christ and live in humble dependence on Him. Lord, give us eyes to see how erectly we prance around. Please enable us to reflect on the righteousness of Christ; that only by His merit imputed to us do we gain admittance to the splendor of heaven. When we come before Your throne of grace in prayer, O Lord, please grant us humble hearts which fall flat at the feet of Jesus in humble love and adoration. Grant that each of us may honestly say, "Nothing in my hands I bring, simply to Thy cross I cling."

True and False Zeal

JOHN NEWTON

Zeal is that pure and heavenly flame,
The fire of love supplies;
While that which often bears the name
Is self in a disguise.

True zeal is merciful and mild,
Can pity and forbear;
The false is headstrong, fierce, and wild,
And breathes revenge and war.

While zeal for truth, the Christian warms,
He knows the worth of peace;
But self contends for names and forms,
Its party to increase.

Zeal has attained its highest aim,
Its end is satisfied,
If sinners love the Savior's name,
Nor seeks it aught beside.

But self, however well employed,
Has its own ends in view,
And says, as boasting Jehu cried,
"Come, see what I can do."

Self may its poor reward obtain,
And be applauded here;
But zeal the best applause will gain
When Jesus shall appear.

Dear Lord, the idol self dethrone,
And from our hearts remove;
And let no zeal by us be shown,
But that which springs from love.

Newton, John. *The Works of the Rev. John Newton.*
Edinburgh: Thomas Nelson, 1841, p. 626.

Pride Lamented

SAMUEL STENNETT

Oft have I turned my eyes within,
And brought to light some latent sin;
But pride, the vice I most detest,
Still lurks securely in my breast.

Here with a thousand arts she tries
To dress me in a fair disguise,
To make a guilty wretched worm
Put on an angel's brightest form.

She hides my follies from mine eyes,
And lifts my virtues to the skies;
And, while the specious tale she tells,
Her own deformity conceals.

Rend, O my God, the veil away,
Bring forth the monster to the day;
Expose her hideous form to view,
And all her restless power subdue.

So shall humility divine
Again possess this heart of mine,
And form a temple for my God,
Which He will make His loved abode.

Stennett, Samuel. *The Works of Samuel Stennett, D.D.*
London: Thomas Tegg, 1824, p. 546.

The Excellency of Man Laid Low before God

RALPH ERSKINE

Shall mortal man, a tainted clod,
Boast righteousness divine;
Or think he can his Maker God,
In purity outshine?

Behold, no trust is put by Him,
In yonder glorious race,
Of bright immortal seraphim,
That stand before His face.

Of folly comparative can He
His purest angels blame,
Who, plunged in His infinity,
Before Him blush for shame?

And shall vain man, in impure state,
His innocence defend?
Will he with his Creator great
Presumptuously contend?

Vile mortal man, a worthless wight,
Triumphs but for a day;
And but inhabits, for a night,
A house of moldering clay.

His strongest lodge and vital fort,
Is founded in the dust,
Which, quickly falling, cuts him short,
And disappoints his trust.

For but how soon a gnawing worm,
Or silly moth assails,
The rampart cannot stand the storm,
The feeble fabric fails.

The sapped foundation every hour
Thus piecemeal feels decay;
And life, even in its blooming flower,
Does daily fade away.

So fast men perish out of sight,
Their pomp that shone before,
And once could wonder fond excite,
Can raise regard no more.

In vain no power and wealth achieved,
For help at last they cry;
For without wisdom, as they lived,
They in their folly die.

Erskine, Ralph. *Erskine's Sermons and Practical Works.*
Aberdeen: A. King & Co., 1863, VII:438-439.

God Magnified by Those That Love His Salvation

PHILIP DODDRIDGE

God of salvation, we adore
Thy saving love, Thy saving power;
And to our utmost stretch of thought,
Hail the redemption Thou hast wrought.

We love the stroke that breaks our chain,
The sword by which our sins are slain;
And while abased in dust we bow,
We sing the grace that lays us low.

Perish each thought of human pride;
Let God alone be magnified.
His glory let the heavens resound,
Shouted from earth's remotest bound.

Saints, who His full salvation know,
Saints, who but taste it here below,
Join every angel's voice to raise.
Continued never-ending praise.

Doddridge, Philip. *The Miscellaneous Works of Philip Doddridge.*
London: Joseph Robinson, 1830, p. 991.

Justification by Faith Alone in Christ's Righteousness

RALPH ERSKINE

Lord, through Thy grace I'll boast no more,
In duties I have done;
I quit the hopes I held before,
And only trust Thy Son.

What was my gain, I for His name,
Do now account my loss;
My former glory is my shame,
I nail it to His cross.

Yea, doubtless, I all things esteem
But loss for Jesus' sake,
That so I may while found in Him,
His righteousness partake.

The choicest service of my hands
Dares not to face Thy throne;
But faith, to answer Thy demands,
Can plead what Christ had done.

Erskine, Ralph. *Erskine's Sermons and Practical Works.*
Aberdeen: A. King & Co., 1863, VII:616.

Meek Redeemer, Now Impart

AUGUSTUS TOPLADY

Lord, I feel a carnal mind
That hangs about me still,
Vainly though I strive to bind
My own rebellious will;
Is not haughtiness of heart,
The gulf between my God and me?
Meek Redeemer, now impart
Thine own humility.

Fain would I my Lord pursue,
Be all my Savior taught,
Do as Jesus bid me do,
And think as Jesus thought;
But 'tis Thou must change my heart,
The perfect gift must come from Thee;
Meek Redeemer, now impart
Thine own humility.

Lord, I cannot, must not, rest,
'Till I Thy mind obtain,
Chase presumption from my breast,
And all Thy mildness gain;
Give me, Lord, Thy gentle heart,
Thy lowly mind my portion be;
Meek Redeemer, now impart
Thine own humility.

Let Thy cross my will control;
Conform me to my Guide.
In Thine image mould my soul,
And crucify my pride;
Give me, Lord, a contrite heart,
A heart that always looks to Thee;
Meek Redeemer, now impart
Thine own humility.

Tear away my every boast,
My stubborn mind abase;
Savior, fix my only trust

In Thy redeeming grace.
Give me a submissive heart,
From pride and self-dependence free;
Meek Redeemer, now impart
Thy own humility.

Toplady, Augustus. *The Works of Augustus Toplady.*
London: J. Chidley, 1837, p. 893.

Humiliation and Praise

JOHN NEWTON

When the wounded spirit hears the voice of Jesus' blood,
How the message stops the tears which else in vain had flowed;
Pardon, grace, and peace proclaimed, and the sinner called a child;
Then the stubborn heart is tamed, renewed and reconciled.

Oh, 'twas grace indeed to spare and save a wretch like me!
Men and angels could not bear what I have offered thee.
Were Thy bolts at their command, hell 'ere now had been my place;
Thou alone couldst silent stand, and wait to show Thy grace.

If, in one created mind, the tenderness and love
Of Thy saints on earth were joined, with all the hosts above;
Still that love were weak and poor, if compared, my Lord, with Thine;
Far too scanty to endure a heart so vile as mine.

Wondrous mercy I have found, but, ah, how faint my praise!
Must I be a cumber-ground, unfruitful all my days?
Do I in Thy garden grow, yet produce Thee only leaves?
Lord, forbid it should be so! The thought my spirit grieves.

Heavy charges Satan brings to fill me with distress;
Let me hide beneath Thy wings, and plead Thy righteousness.
Lord, to Thee for help I call, 'tis Thy promise bids me come;
Tell him Thou hast paid for all, and that shall strike him dumb.

Newton, John. *The Works of the Rev. John Newton.*
Edinburgh: Thomas Nelson, 1841, p. 622.

Christ's Deep Humiliation and High Exaltation

RALPH ERSKINE

All ye that mention Jesus' name,
And are His folk designed,
Submiss was He, be ye the same,
And bear His humble mind.

Who in the form of God did hold
The self-same Deity;
Nor in Him thought it robbery bold,
To equal God most High.

Yet made Himself of no repute,
A mortal likeness wore;
And clothed in human nature's suit,
A servant's form He bore.

Thus even his manhood He suppressed,
Nor made His Godhead shine;
But veiled His glory, and abased,
His majesty divine.

To bear our guilt, exceeding gross,
He stooped exceeding low;
Submiss to death, e'en on the cross,
In all its shame and woe.
God therefore hath exalted Him,
Above the starry frame;
And given Him, on His throne sublime,
A name above every name.

That at His name should every knee,
Bow down, and none rebel;
But own His awful sway to be
O'er heaven, and earth, and hell.

That every tongue confess and blaze,
That Jesus Christ is Lord;
And thus to God, the Father's praise,
The Son may be adored.

Erskine, Ralph. *Erskine's Sermons and Practical Works.*
Aberdeen: A. King & Co., 1863, VII:615-616.

Humbling Ourselves under God's Mighty Hand

PHILIP DODDRIDGE

Beneath Thy mighty hand, O God,
Our souls we prostrate low;
Shine forth with gentle radiant beams,
That we Thy name may know.

Thy hand this various frame produced,
And still supports it well;
That hand with justice and with ease,
Might smite our souls to hell.

Conscious of meanness and of guilt,
We in the dust would lie;
Stretch forth Thy condescending arm,
And lift the humble high.
So in the temples of Thy grace
We'll sovereign mercy own;
And when we shine above the stars,
Extol Thy grace alone.

The more Thou raise such sinful dust,
The lower would it fall;
For less than nothing, Lord, are we,
And Thou art all in all.

Doddridge, Philip. *The Miscellaneous Works of Philip Doddridge.*
London: Joseph Robinson, 1830, p. 1064.

They Keep Crawling Down

MORTIFICATION OF SIN

For you died, and your life is hidden with Christ in God.
When Christ who is our life appears,
Then you also will appear with Him in glory.
Therefore put to death your members which are on the earth:
fornication, uncleanness, passion, evil desire,
And covetousness, which is idolatry.
Because of these things the wrath of God is coming upon
the sons of disobedience, in which you yourselves once walked
when you lived in them.

— COLOSSIANS 3:3-7

They Keep Crawling Down
MORTIFICATION OF SIN

"Every Christian must make up his mind and lay out his life to crucify all his several sins and to keep them crucified, till God has time to have them forever mortified. For, if a malefactor was once arrested and was crucified and was kept crucified till at last he died upon his cross, in that case his days of robbery and murder were at an end. But let the watching soldiers fall asleep, or let them become drunken, and let that crucified criminal's old companions come and take him down from his cross, as sometimes happened, and that rescued malefactor would immediately return to his former crimes and even worse than before. And so will it be with those robbers and murderers who are still alive and unmortified in our own hearts. They may be really and truly be crucified and their days of open and outward transgression may seem to be at an end. But cease watching them; cease for so much as a day or an hour from keeping them crucified, and they will be back that very hour at all their former evil works. Those so besetting sins of yours that are today nailed to their cross and are silent and motionless and shamming death, unless you watch with all your watchfulness they will be down from their cross and will be back again at all their evil ways." (Whyte, Alexander. *Thomas Shepard: Pilgrim Father and Founder of Harvard.* Edinburgh; London: Oliphant Anderson and Ferrier, n.d., p. 142.)

Scripture and our own experience confirm the truth of this quote. We are too quick to take our eyes off a sin we believe has been finally thrust out of our lives. A week or two passes and we are already proudly patting ourselves on the back that this sin has been forever defeated. We even look around in astonishment at other Christians who yet haven't overcome this sin. We should realize that our pride is one of those crucified criminal's old companions who will help the felon down from the cross.

Remember, crucifixion is a very slow form of death. A crucified criminal may live for hours, even days. Christian, be alert, for there is an escape artist ever waiting and watching for your drooping shoulders and sleepy eyes. And if an escape does occur, be quick to use a Scriptural prayer to nail that shameful rascal back on the cross.

Indwelling Sin Lamented

SAMUEL STENNETT

With tears of anguish I lament,
Here at Thy feet, my God,
My passion, pride, and discontent,
And vile ingratitude.

Sure there was ne'er a heart so base,
So false as mine has been;
So faithless to its promises,
So prone to every sin!

My reason tells me Thy commands
Are holy, just, and true;
Tells me whate'er my God demands
Is His most righteous due.

Reason, I hear her counsels weigh,
And all her words approve;
But still I find it hard to obey,
And harder yet to love.

How long, dear Savior, shall I feel
These strugglings in my breast?
When wilt Thou bow my stubborn will,
And give my conscience rest?

Break, sovereign grace, oh, break the charm,
And set the captive free;
Reveal, almighty God, Thine arm,
And haste to rescue me.

Stennett, Samuel. *The Works of Samuel Stennett, D.D.*
London: Thomas Tegg, 1824, pp. 532-533.

After Being Surprised into Sin

AUGUSTUS TOPLADY

Ah, give me, Lord, myself to see,
Against myself to watch and pray;
How weak am I, when left by Thee,
How frail, how apt to fall away!
If but a moment Thou withdraw,
That moment sees me break Thy law.

Jesus, the sinner's only trust,
Let me now feel Thy grace infused!
Ah, raise a captive from the dust,
Nor break a reed already bruised.
Visit me, Lord, in peace again,
Nor let me seek Thy face in vain.

O gracious Lord, now let me find,
Peace and salvation in Thy name;
Be Thou the eyesight of the blind,
The staff and ankles of the lame;
My lifter up whenever I fall,
My strength, my portion, and my all.

Do Thy meek mind descend on me,
Thy Holy Spirit from above;
Assist me, Lord, to follow Thee,
Drawn by the endearing cords of love,
Made perfect by Thy cleansing blood,
Completely saved and born of God.

Toplady, Augustus. *The Works of Augustus Toplady.*
London: J. Chidley, 1837, pp. 889-890.

Dagon before the Ark

JOHN NEWTON

When first to make my heart His own,
The Lord revealed His mighty grace;
Self-reigned like Dagon on the throne,
But could not long maintain its place.

It fell, and owned the power divine—
Grace can with ease the victory gain—
But soon this wretched heart of mine,
Contrived to set it up again.

Again the Lord His name proclaimed,
And brought the hateful idol low;
Then self, like Dagon, broken, maimed,
Seemed to receive a mortal blow.

Yet self is not of life bereft,
Nor ceases to oppose His will;
Though but a maimed stump be left
'Tis Dagon, 'tis an idol still.

Lord, must I always guilty prove,
And idols in my heart have room?
Oh, let the fire of heav'nly love,
The very stump of self consume!

Newton, John. *The Works of the Rev. John Newton.*
Edinburgh: Thomas Nelson, 1841, p. 533.

The Inward Warfare

JOHN NEWTON

Strange and mysterious is my life,
What opposites I feel within—
A stable peace, a constant strife,
The rule of grace, the power of sin;
Too often I am captive led,
Yet daily triumph in my Head.

I prize the privilege of prayer,
But, oh, what backwardness to pray!
Though on the Lord I cast my care,
I feel its burden every day;
I seek His will in all I do,
Yet find my own is working too.

I call the promises my own,
And prize them more than mines of gold.
Yet though their sweetness I have known,
They leave me unimpressed and cold;
One hour upon the truth I feed,
The next I knew not what I read.

I love the holy day of rest,
When Jesus meets His gathered saints;
Sweet day, of all the week the best!
For its return my spirit pants;
Yet often, through my unbelief,
It proves a day of guilt and grief.

While on my Savior I rely,
I know my foes shall lose their aim,
And therefore dare their power defy,
Assured of conquest through His name;
But soon my confidence is slain,
And all my fears return again.

Thus different powers within me strive,
And grace and sin by turns prevail;
I grieve, rejoice, decline, revive,
And victory hangs in doubtful scale.
But Jesus has His promise past,
That grace shall overcome at last.

Newton, John. *The Works of the Rev. John Newton.*
Edinburgh: Thomas Nelson, 1841, pp. 567-568.

Flesh and Spirit

ISAAC WATTS

What different powers of grace and sin
Attend our mortal state!
I hate the thoughts that work within,
And do the works I hate.

Now I complain, and groan, and die,
While sin and Satan reign;
Now raise my songs of triumph high,
For grace prevails again.

So darkness struggles with the light
Till perfect day arise;
Water and fire maintain the fight,
Until the weaker dies.

Thus will the flesh and spirit strive,
And vex and break my peace;
But I shall quit this mortal life,
And sin forever cease.

Watts, Isaac. *The Psalms and Hymns of Isaac Watts.*
Morgan: Soli Deo Gloria Publications, 1997, p. 501.

The Mystery of the Saint's Old and New Man

RALPH ERSKINE

Temptations breed me much annoy,
Yet divers such I count all joy.
On earth I see confusion reel,
Yet wisdom ordering all things well.

I sleep, yet have a waking ear;
I'm blind and deaf, yet see and hear;
Dumb, yet cry, "Abba, Father," plain;
Born only once, yet born again.

My heart's a mirror dim and bright,
A compound strange of day and night;
Of dung and diamonds, dross and gold,
Of summer heat and winter cold.

Down like a stone I sink and dive,
Yet daily upward soar and thrive.
To heaven I fly, to earth I tend;
Still better grow, yet never mend.

My heaven and glory's sure to me,
Though thereof seldom sure I be;
Yet what makes me the surer is,
God is my glory, I am His.

My life's exposed to open view,
Yet closely hid, and known to few,
Some know my place, and whence I came,
Yet neither whence, nor where I am.

I live in earth, which is not odd,
But lo, I also live with God;
A spirit without flesh and blood,
Yet with them both to yield me food.

I live what others live upon,
Yet live I not on bread alone;
But food adapted to my mind,
Bare words, yet not on empty wind.

I'm no anthropophagite rude,
Though fed with human flesh and blood;
But live superlatively fine,
My food's all spirit, all divine.

I feast on fullness night and day,
Yet pinched for want, I pine away;
My leanness, leanness, ah, I cry,
Yet fat and full of sap am I.

As all amphibious creatures do,
I live in land and water too;
To good and evil equal bent,
I'm both a devil and a saint.

While some men who on earth are gods,
Are with the God of heaven at odds;
My heart, where hellish legions are,
Is with the hosts of hell at war.

My will fulfils what's hard to tell,
The counsel both of heaven and hell;
Heaven, without sin, willed sin to be,
Yet will to sin, is sin in me.

To duty seldom I adhere,
Yet to the end I persevere;
I die and rot beneath the clod,
Yet live and reign as long as God.

Erskine, Ralph. *Erskine's Sermons and Practical Works.*
Aberdeen: A. King & Co., 1863, VII:207-208.

For the Kingdom of God

JOHN NORDEN

The God of bliss, who faithful is,
His sacred Word doth send,
To teach us all on Him to call,
And to His laws attend.

His kingdom pure, which shall endure
Forever, doth begin
In those that know how here below
To mortify their sin.

And they that will embrace with skill
The way that trains to bliss,
Shall quickly see that they shall be
Reformed from things amiss.

O God above, look Thou in love
On all that long to see
Thy saving health, Thy heavenly wealth,
And glorious kingdom free.

Thy kingdom show to us below,
That wander here awry;
Direct our feet, Thy statutes sweet,
To us Thy folk decry.

Oh, be not slack, but what we lack,
With speed let us obtain;
For Thou dost feed such as have need,
Thou dost no poor disdain.

Norden, John. *A Progress of Piety.*
Cambridge: Cambridge University Press, 1968, pp. 85-86.

Lord, Give Me Wings

AUGUSTUS TOPLADY

Chained to the world, to sin tied down,
In darkness still I lie;
Lord, break my bonds, Lord, give me wings,
And teach me how to fly.

Instruct my feeble hands to war,
In me Thy strength reveal,
To put my every lust to death,
And fight Thy battles well.

Rend every veil that shades Thy face,
Put on Thine helmet, Lord;
My sin shall fall, my guilt expire,
Beneath Thy conquering sword.

Thou art the mighty God of hosts,
Whose counsels never fail;
Be Thou my glorious Chief, and then
I cannot but prevail.

Toplady, Augustus. *The Works of Augustus Toplady.*
London: J. Chidley, 1837, p. 890 (Poem XXI).

Communing with Our Hearts

PHILIP DODDRIDGE

Return, my roving heart, return,
And chase these shadowy forms no more;
Seek out some solitude to mourn,
And thy forsaken God implore.

Wisdom and pleasure dwell at home—
Retired and silent seek them there;
True conquest is ourselves to overcome.
True strength to break the tempter's snare.

And Thou, my God, whose piercing eye
Distinct surveys each deep recess,
In these abstracted hours draw nigh,
And with Thy presence fill the place.

Through all the mazes of my heart
My search let heavenly wisdom guide,
And still its radiant beams impart,
Till all be searched and purified.

Then, with the visits of Thy love,
Vouchsafe my inmost soul to cheer;
Till every grace shall join to prove,
That God hath fixed His dwelling there.

Doddridge, Philip. *The Miscellaneous Works of Philip Doddridge.*
London: Joseph Robinson, 1830, p. 988.

The Steady Promise

RALPH ERSKINE

Oft earth, and hell, and sin have strove,
To rend my soul from God;
But everlasting is His love,
Sealed with His Darling's blood.

The oath and promise of the Lord
Join to confirm His grace;
Eternal power performs the Word,
And brings the strong solace.

Amid temptations, sharp and long,
I to His refuge flee;
Hope is my anchor, firm and strong,
When storms enrage the sea.

The gospel bears my spirit up;
The never changing God
Lays, for my triple ground of hope,
The Word, the oath, the blood.

Erskine, Ralph. *Erskine's Sermons and Practical Works.*
Aberdeen: A. King & Co., 1863, VII:619.

The Sinner's Rest

AUGUSTUS TOPLADY

Oh, when will Thou my Savior be,
Oh, when shall I be clean,
The true, eternal sabbath see,
A perfect rest from sin?
Jesus, the sinner's rest Thou art,
From guilt, and fear, and pain;
While Thou art absent from my heart,
I look for rest in vain.

The consolations of Thy Word,
My soul hath long upheld,
The faithful promise of the Lord,
Shall surely be fulfilled.
I look to my incarnate God,
Till He His work begin;
And wait till His redeeming blood
Shall cleanse me from all sin.

His great salvation I shall know,
And perfect liberty;
Onward to sin He cannot go,
Whoever abides in Thee.
Added to the Redeemer's fold,
I shall in Him rejoice;
I all His glory shall behold,
And hear my Shepherd's voice.

Oh, that I now the voice might hear,
That speaks my sins forgiv'n;
His Word is past to give me here
The inward pledge of heav'n.
His blood shall over all prevail,
And sanctify the unclean;
The grace that saves from future hell,
Shall save from present sin.

Toplady, Augustus. *The Works of Augustus Toplady.*
London: J. Chidley, 1837, p. 890 (Poem XXII).

Emblem of Eternal Rest

SABBATH

There remains therefore a rest for the people of God.
For He who has entered His rest
Has Himself also ceased from His works,
As God did from His.

— HEBREWS 4:9-10

Emblem of Eternal Rest
SABBATH

The Sabbath began for the Puritans on Saturday evening. This was a time used to examine the week gone by for advances or recessions in their spiritual walk, for prayer, and to read the Scripture. This was done in order to prepare themselves for the coming "market day for their souls." They were in bed early Saturday night so that they were able to rise early on the Sabbath for more soul preparation.

The Puritans viewed the Sabbath as a day when they would meet with God's messenger (the preacher) and hear His Biblical message proclaimed by the power of the Holy Spirit. As it was then, is it not now? Should this visit to the "suburbs of heaven" be seen as anything less?

God has ordained the preaching of the Word, by the power of the Spirit, to be a cure for the ills of the human heart, to lift up Christ, and to humble us under the graciousness of grace. How soon we rob ourselves of that cure, of that "rare and profitable" time by our Sunday afternoon activities such as movies, sports, and shopping.

It has been said that a bee dies when it leaves its sting behind it, but not so a sermon. A sermon only begins to live when its hearer goes home sermon-sick (stung). Sin-sick ransomed sinners, take your prescription correctly; water the sermon by your tears of gratitude and repentance, beseech remembrance of and obedience to the preached Word by your prayers, and digest it slowly by meditation.

Joseph Alleine wrote the following prescription to his congregation: "Pray for the coming of the Spirit in the Word. Come from your knees to the sermon, and come from the sermon to your knees. The sermon does not prosper because it is not watered by prayers and tears, nor covered by meditation." (Alleine, Joseph. *An Alarm to the Unconverted.* Layfayette; Ind: Sovereign Grace Trust Fund, 1990, p. 366.)

Safely through Another Week

JOHN NEWTON

Safely through another week, God has brought us on our way;
Let us now a blessing seek on the approaching Sabbath day,
Day of all the week the best, emblem of eternal rest!

Mercies multiplied each hour through the week our praise demand;
Guarded by almighty power, fed and guided by His hand,
Though ungrateful we have been, only made returns of sin.

While we pray for pardoning grace through the dear Redeemer's name,
Show Thy reconciled face, shine away our sin and shame;
From our worldly care set free, may we rest this night with Thee!

When the morn shall bid us rise, may we feel Thy presence near;
May Thy glory meet our eyes when we in Thy house appear.
There afford us, Lord, a taste of our everlasting feast.

May Thy gospel's joyful sound conquer sinners, comfort saints;
Make the fruits of grace abound, bring relief for all complaints.
Thus may all our Sabbaths prove till we join the church above!

Newton, John. *The Works of the Rev. John Newton.*
Edinburgh: Thomas Nelson, 1841, p. 584.

Blessed Day of God

JOHN MASON

Blessed day of God, most calm, most bright,
The first and best of days;
The laborer's rest, the saint's delight,
A day of mirth and praise.

My Savior's face did make thee shine,
His rising did thee raise;
This made thee heavenly and divine,
Beyond the common days.

The first-fruits do a blessing prove
To all the sheaves behind;
And they that do a Sabbath love,
An happy week shall find.

My Lord on thee His name did fix,
Which makes thee rich and gay;
Amid His golden candlesticks
My Savior walks this day.

He walk in robes, His face shines bright,
The stars are in His hands;
Out of His mouth, that place of might,
A two-edged sword doth stand.

Graced with our Lord's appearance thus,
As well as with His name,
Thou mayest demand respect from us,
Upon a double claim.

This day God doth His vessels broach,
His conduits run with wine;
He that loves not this day's approach
Scorns heaven and Savior-shine.

What slaves are those who slavery choose,
And garlic for their feast;
While milk and honey they refuse,
And the Almighty's rest!

This market day doth saints enrich,
And smiles upon them all;
It is their Pentecost, on which
The Holy Ghost doth fall.

Oh, day of wonders, mercy's dawn,
The weary soul's recruit;
The Christian's Goshen, heaven's dawn,
The bud of endless fruit!

Oh, could I love as I have loved
Thy watches heretofore;
As England's glory thou hast proved,
Mayest thou be so yet more.

This day must I for God appear,
For, Lord, the day is Thine;
Oh, let me spend it in Thy fear,
Then shall the day be mine.

Cease work and play, throughout the day,
That I to God may rest;
Now let me talk with God, and walk
With God, and I am blessed.

Mason, John. *Spiritual Songs, or Songs of Praise to Almighty God.*
Edinburgh: James Taylor, 1880, pp. 65-67.

The Lord's Day
(Delight in Ordinances)

ISAAC WATTS

Welcome, sweet day of rest,
That saw the Lord arise;
Welcome to this reviving breast,
And these rejoicing eyes!

The King Himself comes near,
And feasts His saints today;
Here we may sit, and see Him here,
And love, and praise, and pray.

One day amid the place
Where my dear God hath been,
Is sweeter than ten thousand days
Of pleasurable sin.

My willing soul would stay
In such a frame as this,
And sit, and sing herself away
To everlasting bliss.

Watts, Isaac. *The Psalms and Hymns of Isaac Watts.*
Morgan: Soli Deo Gloria Publications, 1997, pp. 411-412.

The Enjoyment of Christ
(Delight in Worship)
ISAAC WATTS

Far from my thoughts, vain world, be gone,
Let my religious hours alone;
Fain would my eyes my Savior see;
I wait a visit, Lord, from Thee.

My heart grows warm with holy fire,
And kindles with a pure desire;
Come, my dear Jesus, from above,
And feed my soul with heavenly love.

The trees of life immortal stand,
In fragrant rows at Thy right hand;
And in sweet murmurs, by their side,
Rivers of bliss perpetual glide.

Haste, then, but with a smiling face,
And spread the table of Thy grace;
Bring down a taste of fruit divine,
And cheer my heart with sacred wine.

Blessed Jesus, what delicious fare;
How sweet Thy entertainments are!
Never did angels taste above
Redeeming grace, and dying love.

Hail, great Immanuel, all divine!
In Thee Thy Father's glories shine;
Thou brightest, sweetest, fairest One,
That eyes have seen or angels known.

Watts, Isaac. *The Psalms and Hymns of Isaac Watts.*
Morgan: Soli Deo Gloria Publications, 1997, p. 412.

To the Holy Spirit

AUGUSTUS TOPLADY

Come, Holy Spirit, our souls inspire,
And warm with uncreated fire!
Thou the anointing Spirit art,
Who dost thy sevenfold gift impart;
Thy blessed unction from above
Is comfort, life, and fire of love.

Enable with perpetual light
The dullness of our blinded sight;
Anoint and cheer us all our days,
With the abundance of Thy grace;
Our foes convert, give peace at home;
Where Thou art guide, no ill can come.

Teach us to know the Father, Son,
And thee; a Trinity in one,
That, through the ages all along,
This may be our endless song;
Praise to Thy eternal love—
Father, Son, and mystic Dove!

Toplady, Augustus. *The Works of Augustus Toplady.*
London: J. Chidley, p. 908.

A Praise of God's Favor in Protecting His Church

JOHN NORDEN

Our God is good; why should we then
So long neglect His praise?
His help doth pass the help of men,
Whose laws and love decays.
But lo, the love of God endures,
From day to day it stands;
His spouse to love and live He lures,
And breaks her cruel bands.

He sends His Word and gives her light;
His gospel feeds His flock.
His people only take their flight
To Him their lively Rock.
On Him they stay, on Him they stand,
And He extends His aid;
He breaks with truth the doleful band,
Whereat His church dismayed.

No pompous pope, no Spaniard proud,
No direful drum of foe,
No shaft, no shot, no rainless cloud,
Can daunt His spouse with woe.
What though the peevish man of sin
His bloody badge display?
What if he vainly vaunt to win?
Be still—he shall decay.

The proudest of our foes shall fall,
Their stoutest strength shall rue;
The stately strumpet, fraught with gall,
Shall faint, and all her crew.

Jehovah yet His church shall save,
And with His hand defend;
Who then will rest a popish slave,
And not our England's friend?

Breathe out Thy word, O God, our guide;
Let it be published so,
That it may stand and still abide,
And teach Thy church to grow.
Let truth prevail, let faith abound,
Let all reform their ways;
Our queen preserve, her foes confound;
Send peace in all her days.

Norden, John. *A Progress of Piety.*
Cambridge: Cambridge University Press, 1968, pp. 104-105.

The Joy of Church Fellowship Rightfully Attended

EDWARD TAYLOR

In heaven soaring up, I dropped an ear
On earth, and, oh, sweet melody!
And listening, found it was the saints who were
Encoached for heaven that sang for joy.
For in Christ's coach they sweetly sing,
As they to glory ride therein.

Oh, joyous hearts, enfired with holy flame,
Is speech thus tasseled with praise?
Will not your inward fire of joy contain,
That it in open flames doth blaze?
For in Christ's coach saints sweetly sing,
As they to glory ride therein.

And if a string do slip by chance,
They soon do screw it up again; whereby
They set it in a more melodious tune
And a diviner harmony.
For in Christ's coach they sweetly sing,
As they to glory ride therein.

In all their acts, public and private, nay,
And secret too, they praise impart.
But in their acts divine, and worship, they
With hymns do offer up their heart.
Thus in Christ's coach they sweetly sing,
As they to glory ride therein.

Some few not in; and some whose time and place
Block up this coach's way, do go
As travellers afoot; and so do trace
The road that gives them right thereto;
While in this coach these sweetly sing,
As they to glory ride therein.

Taylor, Edward. *Early New England Meditative Poetry.*
New York: Paulist Press, 1988, pp. 156-157.

The Lord's Day

JOHN NEWTON

How welcome to the saints, when pressed
With six days noise, and care, and toil,
Is the returning day of rest,
Which hides them from the world a while.

Now, from the throng withdrawn away,
They seem to breathe a different air;
Composed and softened by the day,
All things another aspect wear.

How happy if their lot is cast,
Where statedly the gospel sounds;
The Word is honey to their taste,
Renews their strength, and heals their wounds.

Though pinched with poverty at home,
With sharp afflictions daily fed,
It makes amends, if they can come
To God's own house for heavenly bread.

With joy they hasten to the place
Where they their Savior oft have met;
And while they feast upon His grace,
Their burdens and their griefs forget.

This favored lot, my friends, is ours;
May we the privilege improve,
And find these consecrated hours
Sweet earnests of the joys above!

We thank Thee for Thy day, oh Lord;
Here we Thy promised presence seek;
Open Thine hand, with blessings stored,
And give us manna for the week.

Newton, John. *The Works of the Rev. John Newton.*
Edinburgh: Thomas Nelson, 1841, p. 586.

The Pleasures of Worship

SAMUEL STENNETT

How charming is the place,
Where my Redeemer God
Unveils the beauties of His face,
And sheds His love abroad!

Not the fair palaces,
To which the great resort,
Are once to be compared with this,
Where Jesus holds His court.

Here, on the mercy seat,
With radiant glory crowned,
Our joyful eyes behold Him sit,
And smile on all around.

To Him their prayers and cries
Each humble soul presents;
He listens to their broken sighs,
And grants them all their wants.

To them His sovereign will
He graciously imparts;
And in return accepts, with smiles,
The tribute of their hearts.

Give me, O Lord, a place
Within Thy blessed abode,
Among the children of Thy grace,
The servants of my God.

Stennett, Samuel. *The Works of Samuel Stennett, D.D.*
London: Thomas Tegg, 1824, p. 547.

A Psalm of Praise

RICHARD BAXTER

Ye holy angels bright, who stand before God's throne
And dwell in glorious light, praise ye the Lord each one.
Assist our song, or else the theme too high doth seem for mortal tongue.
Ye blessed souls at rest, that see your Savior's face,
Whose glory, e'en the least, is far above our grace.

God's praises sound, as in His sight
With sweet delight you do abound.
Ye saints, who toil below, adore your heavenly King,
And onward as ye go, some joyful anthem sing;
Take what He gives, and praise Him still, through good or ill,
    who ever lives!

All nations of the earth, extol the world's great King;
With melody and mirth His glorious praises sing,
For He still reigns, and will bring low the proudest foe that Him disdains.
Sing forth Jehovah's praise, ye saints that on Him call!
Him magnify always, His holy churches all!

In Him rejoice, and there proclaim His holy name with sounding voice.
My soul, bear thou thy part, triumph in God above,
And with a well tuned heart sing thou the songs of love.
And all my days, let no distress nor fears suppress His joyful praise.

Away, distrustful care! I have Thy promise, Lord,
To banish all despair, I have Thine oath and Word,
And therefore I shall see Thy face and there Thy grace shall magnify.
With Thy triumphant flock then I shall numbered be;
Built on th'eternal Rock, His glory shall we see.

The heav'ns so high, with praise shall ring,
And all shall sing in harmony.

Baxter, Richard. *Poetical Fragments by Richard Baxter.*
W. Germany: Gregg International Publishers Limited, 1971, pp. 85-88.

On the Lord's Day

JOHN MASON

Thou spreadest a weekly table, Lord,
Where souls may banquet on Thy Word;
While means and plenty we enjoy,
Let not our souls be parched and dry.

We wait here at Bethesda's pool,
Those waters which refresh and cool;
We wait, whose souls are scorched with sin,
Oh, come, dear Savior, help us in.

Thy power and Thy grace display,
Be Thou among us on Thy day;
That sinners may observe Thy call,
And numerous converts to Thee fall.

That those who do Thy footsteps trace,
May find all sweetness in Thy grace;
Oh, may they never more complain
That they have sought their God in vain.

Thy people at Thy footstool lie,
Behold us with a gracious eye;
Oh, let our souls with Jesus meet,
Our fellowship with Him be sweet.

Among Thy people here am I,
Lord, let me not be passed by;
Let this poor soul with triumph say,
"I've seen my dearest Lord today."

I sit within Thy temple shade,
Oh, let Thy presence make me glad;
Love me, my Lord, or else I die,
Thy love alone can satisfy.

Mason, John. *Spiritual Songs, or Songs of Praise to Almighty God.*
Edinburgh: James Taylor, 1880, pp. 163-165.

A Place for Prayer

JOHN NEWTON

O Lord, our languid souls inspire,
For here we trust Thou art;
Send down a coal of heavenly fire,
To warm each waiting heart.

Dear Shepherd of Thy people, hear,
Thy presence now display;
As Thou hast given a place for prayer,
So give us hearts to pray.

Show us some tokens of Thy love,
Our fainting hope to raise,
And pour Thy blessings from above,
That we may render praise.

Within these walls let holy peace,
And love and concord dwell;
Here give the troubled conscience ease
The wounded spirit heal.

The feeling heart, the melting eye,
The humbled mind bestow;
And shine upon us from on high,
To make our graces grow.

May we in faith receive Thy Word,
In faith present our prayers;
And, in the presence of our Lord,
Unbosom all our cares.

And may the gospel's joyful sound,
Enforced by mighty grace,
Awaken many sinners round,
To come and fill the place.

Newton, John. *The Works of the Rev. John Newton.*
Edinburgh: Thomas Nelson, 1841, pp. 585-586.

King of Glory

NATHANIEL VINCENT

King of glory, King of peace,
I will love Thee;
And that love may never cease,
I will move Thee.

Thou hast granted my request,
Thou hast heard me;
Thou didst note my working breast,
Thou hast spared me.

Wherefore with my utmost art,
I will sing Thee;
And the cream of all my heart,
I will bring Thee.

Though my sins against me cried,
Thou didst clear me;
And alone, when they replied,
Thou didst hear me.

Seven whole days, not one in seven,
I will praise Thee;
In my heart, though not in heaven,
I can raise Thee.

Thou grewest soft and moist with tears,
Thou relented;
And when justice called for fears,
Thou dissented.

Small it is in this poor sort
To enroll Thee;
Even eternity is too short
To extol Thee.

Vincent, Nathaniel. *The True Touchstone Which Shows Both Grace and Nature.*
London, 1681, pp. 335-336.

A Psalm of Praise for the Lord's Day

WILLIAM BURKITT

This is the day, the Lord's own day,
A day of holy rest;
Oh, teach our souls to rest from sin,
That rest will please Thee best.

This is the day, Thy day, O Lord,
On which Thou didst arise;
For sinners having made Thyself
A sinless sacrifice.

Thou, Thou alone, redeemed hast
Our souls from deadly thrall;
With no less price than Thine own blood,
The purchase of us all.

Had Thou not died, we had not lived,
But died eternally;
We'll live to Him that died for us,
And praise His name on high.

Thou died and Thou did rise again,
And did ascend on high,
That we poor sinners, lost and dead,
Might live eternally.

Thy blood was shed instead of ours;
Thy soul our guilt did bear.
Thou took our sins upon Thyself,
Thy love's beyond compare.

How dear and welcome, Lord, to me
Is Thy most holy day!
But what a Sabbath shall I keep
For evermore with Thee?

I come, I wait, I hear, I pray;
Thy footsteps, Lord, I trace.
I joy to think this is the way
To see my Savior's face.

These are my preparation days,
And when my soul is dressed,
These Sabbaths shall deliver me
To mine eternal rest.

Burkitt, William. *An Help and Guide to Christian Families.*
London: Longman, Hurst, and Co. and J. Mawman, 1822, pp. 141-142.

The Eternal Sabbath

PHILIP DODDRIDGE

Lord of the Sabbath, hear our vows,
On this Thy day, in this Thy house,
And own, as grateful sacrifice,
The songs, which from the desert rise.

Thine earthly Sabbaths, Lord, we love,
But there's a nobler rest above;
To that our laboring souls aspire
With ardent pangs of strong desire.

No more fatigue, no more distress,
Nor sin nor hell shall reach the place;
No groans to mingle with the songs,
Which warble from immortal tongues.

 No rude alarms of raging foes;
No cares to break the long repose;
No midnight shade, no clouded sun,
But sacred, high, eternal noon.

Oh, long-expected day, begin;
Dawn on these realms of woe and sin.
Fain would we leave this weary road,
And sleep in death to rest with God.

Doddridge, Philip. *The Miscellaneous Works of Philip Doddridge.*
London: Joseph Robinson, 1830, p. 1057.

Taking Careful Aim

POEMS FOR YOUTH

For the Lord gives wisdom;
From His mouth come knowledge and understanding.

— PROVERBS 2:6

Taking Careful Aim
POEMS FOR YOUTH

"I beseech your Lordship to begin now to frame your love, and to cast it in no mold but one, that it may be for Christ only; for when your love is now in the framing and making, it will take best with Christ ... Promise the lodging of your soul first away to Christ, and stand by your first covenant, and keep to Jesus, that He may find you honest. It is easy to master an arrow, and to set it right, ere the string be drawn; but when once it is shot, and in the air, and the flight begun, then ye have no more power at all to command it." (Rutherford, Samuel. *Letters of Samuel Rutherford.* Edinburgh: Banner of Truth, 1984, pp. 460-461.)

Samuel Rutherford rightly recognizes that youth is the time when the arrows are aimed and the bow is drawn with choices and decisions which will affect the future. If young people would but take a moment and look around, what lessons they could learn from the flight of arrows which have been aimed incorrectly. An arrow which has hit its sinful target will cause many painful days on this earth not only for the archer but for family and friends as well. A lifetime of trying to catch that arrow and desiring a second aim will not make it happen.

As regret-filled archers, we are thankful that we have a gracious Instructor. When we turn our bow and our remaining arrows over to Him, He enables us to aim and shoot correctly. Be sure your face is in the right direction and your aim well taken. Let not anyone or anything take your eye off the bull's-eye, Jesus Christ.

A Prayer for Youth

JOHN NEWTON

Bestow, dear Lord, upon our youth,
The gift of saving grace;
And let the seed of sacred truth
Fall in a fruitful place.

Grace is a plant, where'er it grows,
Of pure and heavenly root;
But fairest in the youngest shows,
And yields the sweetest fruit.

Ye careless ones, oh hear betimes
The voice of sovereign love;
Your youth is stained with many crimes,
But mercy reigns above.

True, you are young, but there's a stone
Within the youngest breast,
Or half the crimes which you have done,
Would rob you of your rest.

For you the public prayer is made,
Oh, join the public prayer!;
For you the sacred tear is shed,
Oh, shed yourselves a tear!

We pray that you may early prove
The Spirit's power to teach;
You cannot be too young to love
That Jesus whom we preach.

Newton, John. *The Works of the Rev. John Newton.*
Edinburgh: Thomas Nelson, 1841, pp. 574-575.

Regard to Scripture
Pressed Upon Young Persons

PHILIP DODDRIDGE

Indulgent God, with pitying eye
The sons of men survey,
And see how youthful sinners sport
In a destructive way.

Ten thousand dangers lurk around,
To bear them to the tomb;
Each in an hour may plunge them down,
Where hope can never come.

Reduce, O Lord, their wandering minds,
Amused with airy dreams,
That heavenly wisdom may dispel
Their visionary schemes.

With holy caution may they walk,
And be Thy word their guide;
Till each, the desert safely passed,
On Zion's hill abide.

Doddridge, Philip. *The Miscellaneous Works of Philip Doddridge.*
London: Joseph Robinson, 1830, p. 996.

Answering to Their Kind

JOHN FLAVEL

It would be a strange and monstrous thing to see
Cherries or plumbs grow on an apple tree.
Whoever gathered from the thistle figs?
Or fruitless grapes from off the worthless twigs
Of pricking thorns? In nature still we find,
All its productions answering to their kind.

As are the plants we set, or seeds we sow,
Such is the fruit we shake, and corn we mow.
And canst thou think, that from corruption's root
Thy soul shall pluck the sweet and pleasant fruit

Of spiritual peace? Whoever that was wise,
Amused himself with such absurdities?
Look what you sow, the very same you'll reap,
The fruit of what you plant, be sure you'll eat,
How are they baffled by a subtle devil,
Who hope for heaven, while their ways are evil?
Such reasonings here their credulous souls beguile,
At which, in other things, themselves would smile.
Our present acts, though slightly passed by,
Are so much seed sown for eternity.

The seeds of prayers, secret groans and tears,
Will shoot at last into the full-blown ears
Of peace and joy. Blessed are they that sow,
Beside these waters, yea, thrice blessed, that go,
Bearing such precious seed. Though now they mourn,
With joyful sheaves they shortly shall return.
Needs must the full-ripe fruits in heaven be good,
When as the seed was glory in the bud.
But oh, the bitter, baneful fruits of sin,
When all the pleasures sinners have therein,

Like faded blossoms to the ground shall fall,
Then they will taste the wormwood and the gall!
What God and conscience now of sin report,
You slight, and with their dreadful threatenings sport;
But He'll convince you then your ways are naught,
As Gideon the men of Succoth taught.
If sermons cannot, fire and brimstone must
Teach men how good it is to pamper lust.
When conscience takes thee by the throat, and cries,
"Now wretch, now sinner, thou that didst despise

My warnings; learn, and ever learning be,
"That lesson which thou never wouldst learn of me."
The stoutest sinner then would howl and roar,
Oh, sin, I never saw thy face before.

Is this the fruit of sin? Is this the place
Where I must lie? Is this indeed the case
Of my poor soul? Must I be bound in chains
With these companions? Oh, are these the gains,
I get by sin? Poor wretch—I that would never
See this before, am now undone forever!

Flavel, John. *The Works of John Flavel.*
London: The Banner of Truth Trust, 1968, V:125-126 (The Poem).

Waiting at Wisdom's Gates

JOHN NEWTON

Ensnared too long my heart has been in folly's hurtful ways;
Oh, may I now, at length, begin to hear what Wisdom says!

'Tis Jesus, from the mercy-seat, invites me to His rest;
He calls poor sinners to His feet to make them truly blessed.

Approach, my soul, to Wisdom's gates while it is called today;
No one who watches there, and waits shall e'er be turned away.

He will not let me seek in vain, for all who trust His Word
Shall everlasting life obtain, and favor from the Lord.

Lord, I have hated Thee too long, and dared Thee to Thy face;
I've done my soul exceeding wrong in slighting all Thy grace.

Now I would break my league with death, and live to Thee alone;
Oh, let Thy Spirit's seal of faith secure me for Thine own.

Let all the saints assembled here, yes, let all heav'n rejoice,
That I began with this new year to make the Lord my choice.

Newton, John. The Works of the Rev. John Newton.
Edinburgh: Thomas Nelson, 1841, p. 579.

The Encouragement Young Persons Have to Seek and to Love Christ

PHILIP DODDRIDGE

Ye hearts, with youthful vigor warm,
In smiling crowds draw near,
And turn from every mortal charm,
A Savior's voice to hear.

He, Lord of all the worlds on high,
Stoops to converse with you;
And lays His radiant glories by,
Your friendship to pursue.

"The soul, that longs to see My face,
Is sure My love to gain;
And those that early seek My grace,
Shall never seek in vain."

What object, Lord, my soul should move,
If once compared with Thee?
What beauty should command my love,
Like what in Christ I see?

Away, ye false delusive toys,
Vain tempters of the mind!
'Tis here I fix my lasting choice,
And here true bliss I find.

Doddridge, Philip. *The Miscellaneous Works of Philip Doddridge.*
London: Joseph Robinson, 1830, p. 1000.

Early Piety

SAMUEL STENNETT

How soft the words my Savior speaks!
How kind the promises He makes!
A bruised reed He never breaks,
Nor will He quench the smoking flax.

The humble poor He won't despise,
Nor on the contrite sinner frown;
His ear is open to their cries,
He quickly sends salvation down.

When piety in early minds,
Like tender buds, begins to shoot,
He guards the plants from threatening winds,
And ripens blossoms into fruit.

With humble souls He bears a part,
In all the sorrows they endure;
Tender and gracious is His heart,
His promise is forever sure.

He sees the struggles that prevail,
Between the powers of grace and sin;
He kindly listens while they tell
The bitter pangs they feel within.

Though pressed with fears on every side,
They know not how the strife may end;
Yet He will soon the cause decide,
And judgment unto victory send.

Stennett, Samuel. *The Works of Samuel Stennett, D.D.*
London: Thomas Tegg, 1824, p. 551.

Youth

BENJAMIN KEACH

Tis not for riches, nor for pleasure here,
Nor honors, which by men so prized are;
Nor length of days, Lord, do I seek, or crave,
'Tis something else my soul doth long to have.
The earth's a blast, and all the world's a bubble,
There's nothing in it can ease me of my trouble.
Such is my state, nought but Thy hands can save,
'Tis Thou must raise dead Lazarus from the grave.
Knock off these bolts, and set Thy prisoner free,
And give Thy grace, Lord Jesus, unto me.

My fainting spirits comfort and refresh,
Oh, spare my soul, but crucify the flesh;
Complete Thy work, Lord Jesus, on my heart,
And Thy own righteousness to me impart.
There's nought, I see, will do me any good,
But the dear merits of Thy precious blood.
My bleeding soul will faint away and die,
If Thou dost not Thy blood with speed apply.
How hath my panting breast sent many a groan,
With bitter tears up to Thy gracious throne,

For one sweet look, and aspect of Thine eye;
There's nothing else that will me satisfy.
Oh, manifest Thy love unto my soul,
For that will cure me, and soon make me whole.
My great request, alas, is only this,
Come, seal Thy love to me with a sweet kiss;
For nought is there on earth, or heaven above,
Which I esteem, or value like Thy love,
A promise grant, some word to rely on,
Before my life and little hopes be gone.

My soul's afraid, and trembles, Thou mayst see,
Because I know that I unworthy be.
How did I grieve, and put my soul in pain;
The thoughts of which doth cut my heart in twain.
Thy messengers, how did my soul refuse,
And did poor conscience wickedly abuse,
Who did receive commission from above,
Either to clear, or sharply to reprove?
I unto truth oft-times turned a deaf ear,
And unto Satan rather did adhere.

I slighted Thee, and sin I did embrace,
Which makes me blush to view Thy heavenly face.
If Thou shouldst pardon such a one as I,
And save my soul to all eternity;
And me embrace in a contract of love,
And all Thy wrath forever quite remove;
It would be grace, and love beyond degree,
And such which never can expressed be.
Oh, wilt thou speak again, dear Savior do;
A promise, Lord, or I'll not let Thee go.

Keach, Benjamin. *War with the Devil.*
London: E. Johnston, 1771, pp. 75-76.

Earthly Prospects Deceitful

JOHN NEWTON

Oft in vain the voice of truth,
Solemnly and loudly warns;
Thoughtless, unexperienced youth,
Though it hears, the warning scorns.
Youth in fancy's glass surveys
Life prolonged to distant years,
While the vast imagined space,
Filled with sweets and joys appears.

Awful disappointment soon
O'erclouds the prospect gay;
Some their sun goes down at noon,
Torn by death's strong hand away.
Where are then their pleasing schemes?
Where the joys they hope to find?
Gone forever, like their dreams,
Leaving not a trace behind.

Others, who are spared a while,
Live to weep o'er fancy's cheat;
Find distress, and pain, and toil,
Bitter things instead of sweet.
Sin has spread a curse around,
Poisoned all things here below;
On this base polluted ground,
Peace and joy can never grow.

Grace alone can cure our ills,
Sweeten life with all its cares;
Regulate our stubborn wills,
Save us from surrounding snares.
Though you oft have heard in vain,
Former years in folly spent,
Grace invites you yet again,
Once more calls you to repent.

Called again, at length, beware,
Hear the Savior's voice, and live;
Lest He in His wrath should swear,
He no more will warning give.
Pray that you may hear and feel,
Ere the day of grace be past;
Lest your hearts grow hard as steel,
Or this year should prove your last.

Newton, John. *The Works of the Rev. John Newton.*
Edinburgh: Thomas Nelson, 1841, p. 574.

The World

JOHN NEWTON

See, the world for youth prepares,
Harlot-like, her gaudy snares;
Pleasures round her seem to wait,
But 'tis all a painted cheat.

Rash and unsuspecting youth,
Thinks to find thee always smooth,
Always kind, till better taught,
By experience dearly bought.

So the calm, but faithless sea,
(Lively emblem, world, of thee,)
Tempts the shepherd from the shore,
Foreign regions to explore.

While no wrinkled wave is seen,
While the sky remains serene,
Filled with hopes and golden schemes,
Of a storm he little dreams.

Before too long the tempest raves,
Then he trembles at the waves;
Wishes then he had been wise,
But too late he sinks and dies.

Hapless thus are they, vain world,
Soon on rocks of ruin hurled,
Who admiring thee, untried,
Court thy pleasure, wealth, or pride.

Such a shipwreck had been mine,
Had not Jesus—name divine!—
Saved me with a mighty hand,
And restored my soul to land,

Now, with gratitude I raise
Ebenezers to His praise,
Now my rash pursuits are o'er,
I can trust thee, world, no more.

Newton, John. *The Works of the Rev. John Newton.*
Edinburgh: Thomas Nelson, 1841, p. 603.

For God's Direction in our Callings

JOHN NORDEN

O God of gods, O Father great,
Thou Guide of all degrees;
The high and low look up to Thee,
Attendant on their knees.

We have our being and our food,
Our wisdom and our skill,
Our high estate, all honor eke,
And callings, at Thy will.

All kings receive their scepters pure,
And diadems for Thee;
Thou make them apt to rule a land,
Else they unable be.

Thou givest sage and sacred men,
And senators most grave,
To guide Thy people in the hests,
That fit them best to have.

Thou choosest eke the godliest ones,
And meetest men to be,
The preachers of Thy sacred will,
Who learn to teach from Thee.

Thy grace doth guide their lips aright,
Else speak they all awry;
Thou art the Fountain full of love,
Whereof they drink, or die.

The poorest Thou dost frame to skill,
The lowest learns to live;
Each hand takes hold of art from Thee—
Thou dost all blessings give.

Else all their curious cunning fails,
Our labors lose their grace;
In vain we travail, and our toil
Turns us to poorest place.

Sith then, good Father, each degree
Depends on Thee for aid,
The high and low, wealthy and wise;
Else rest they all unstaid.

Bless all Thy people in their charge,
Our callings all direct;
Teach prince and people in the way
That graceth Thine elect.

Norden, John. *A Progress of Piety.*
Cambridge: Cambridge University Press, 1968, pp. 133-134.

The Forest of Death

PILGRIMS ON EARTH

While we do not look at the things which are seen,
But at the things which are not seen.
For the things which are seen are temporary,
But the things which are not seen are eternal.

— 2 CORINTHIANS 4:18

The Forest of Death
PILGRIMS ON EARTH

"Build your nest upon no tree here; for God hath sold this whole forest to death; and every tree whereupon we would rest is ready to be cut down, to the end we may fly and mount up, and build upon the Rock, and dwell in the holes of the Rock." (Rutherford, Samuel. *Letters of Samuel Rutherford*. Edinburgh; Carlisle: Banner of Truth, 1984, p. 41.)

We may pity the foolishness of a bird building her nest in a tree about to be cleared away by a construction crew. And yet are we not as foolish as she? Often, we too build our nests—cast our hopes—on temporal things which the Lord has said will be burned up on the last day.

What trees grow in this temporal forest? Trees of fame and fortune. Trees of cars and houses. Trees of foolish amusements and entertainment. Trees of endless degrees and honorariums. Caution! These trees are marked for destruction. Build not your nest in them.

Though difficult, thankful we should be when the divine Woodsman's axe causes our doomed tree to come crashing down, making us flee to and hide in the cleft of the Rock. In this safe, sure dwelling place should rest our imperishable nest.

Contempt of the World

AUGUSTUS TOPLADY

Can ought below engross my thought,
Or am I to the world confined?
Nay, let my pure affections soar
To objects of a nobler kind.

I know I'm but a pilgrim here,
That seeks a better, promised land.
Then may I run and never tire,
Till that celestial home's obtained.

Resolved to tread the sacred way
That Jesus watered with His blood,
I bend my fixed and cheerful course
Through that rough path my Master trod.

Contemptuous of the world I live,
A daily death rejoice to die;
And, while I move and walk below,
My absent heart mounts up on high.

O Light of life, still guide my steps,
Without Thy friendly aid I stray;
Lead me, my God, for I am blind,
Direct me, and point out my way.

Let the vain world applaud or frown,
Still may I heaven's path pursue;
Still may I stand unshook, and keep
The center of my hopes in view.

Though Satan, earth, and self oppose,
Yet, through Thy help I'll persevere;
To Canaan's hills my eyes lift up,
And choose my lot and portion there.

The way that leads to glory lies
Through ill report, contempt, and loss;
Assist me to deny myself,
To follow Thee and bear Thy cross.

Let Satan never come between,
Nor separate my God from me;
But may my soul, in every storm,
Find a sure resting place in Thee.

Toplady, Augustus. *The Works of Augustus Toplady.*
London: J. Chidley, 1837, p. 906.

Vanity of the World

SAMUEL STENNETT

In vain the giddy world inquires,
Forgetful of their God,
"Who will supply our vast desires,
Or show us any good?"

Through the wide circuit of the earth
Their eager wishes rove,
In chase of honor, wealth, and mirth,
The phantoms of their love.

But oft these shadowy joys elude
Their most intense pursuit;
Or, if they seize the fancied good,
There's poison in the fruit.

Lord, from this world call off my love,
Set my affections right;
Bid me aspire to joys above,
And walk no more by sight.

Oh, let the glories of Thy face
Upon my bosom shine;
Assured of Thy forgiving grace,
My joys will be divine.

Stennett, Samuel. *The Works of Samuel Stennett, D.D.*
London: Thomas Tegg, 1824, p. 548.

The Enchantment Dissolved

JOHN NEWTON

Blinded in youth by Satan's arts,
The world to our unpracticed hearts,
A flattering prospect shows;
Our fancy forms a thousand schemes
Our gay delights and golden dreams,
And undisturbed repose.

So in the desert's dreary waste,
By magic power produced in haste—
As ancient fables say—
Castles, and groves, and music sweet,
The senses of the traveller meet,
And stop him in his way.

But while he listens with surprise,
The charm dissolves, the vision dies,
'Twas but enchanted ground.
Thus, if the Lord our spirit touch,
The world, which promised us much,
A wilderness is found.

At first we start, and feel distressed,
Convinced we never can have rest
In such a wretched place;

But He whose mercy breaks the charm,
Reveals His own almighty arm,
And bids us seek His face.

Then we begin to live indeed,
When from our sin and bondage freed,
By this beloved Friend;
We follow Him from day to day,
Assured of grace through all the way
And glory at the end.

Newton, John. *The Works of the Rev. John Newton.*
Edinburgh: Thomas Nelson, 1841, p. 603.

The World's Three Chief Temptations

ISAAC WATTS

When in the light of faith divine,
We look on things below—
Honor, and gold, and sensual joy,
How vain and dangerous too!

Honor's a puff of noisy breath,
Yet men expose their blood,
And venture everlasting death,
To gain that airy good.

While others starve the nobler mind,
And feed on shining dust,
They rob the serpent of his food
To indulge a sordid lust.

The pleasures that allure our sense
Are dangerous snares to souls;
There's but a drop of flattering sweet,
And dashed with bitter bowls.

God is my all-sufficient good,
My portion and my choice;
In Him my vast desires are filled,
And all my powers rejoice.

In vain the world accosts my ear,
And tempts my heart anew;
I cannot buy your bliss so dear,
Nor part with heaven for you.

Watts, Isaac. *The Psalms and Hymns of Isaac Watts.*
Morgan: Soli Deo Gloria Publications, 1997, pp. 475-476.

A True Denial of Ourselves

JOHN NORDEN

Corrupt and filthy are we all,
The proudest man is dust;
No comfort here—we live in thrall—
And linger here in lust.
The sweetest of delights that we
Can choose to please our will,
What brings it us? Who doth not see
That pleasures turn to ill?

Art thou a man whose state is great,
If pomp exalt thy mind,
What then, thy soul with sin impleat,
Bewrays thy pleasures blind.
A doleful bell doth wait to ring,
When thou secure shalt die;
What son of glory canst thou sing,
When corpse in grave shall lie?

What shall avail thy lofty looks,
Where at the poor do quake?
And what thy Machavilian books,
Whose cursed sleights forsake?
Thy bravest buildings high in state,
Thy golden god's but dust;
Thy Thrasos and thy Gnathos mate,
Nor more shall serve thy lust.

Thy formal friends, that fawn on thee,
And please the time for gain,
Will sigh in show, but shrink from thee,
When most thou groan in pain.
Thy rich array, which here doth make
Thy stinking carcass gay,
Thy foe, when thou art gone, will take,
And laugh, and thou in clay.

No state so strong, no man so sure,
No office, or degree,
Can grant us warrant to endure
Beyond our time, we see.
Why then doth flesh triumph, and brave
Itself in pleasing days?
Yet sinks in sins, at last the grave,
Our gross farewell displays.

Oh, then in haste and happy time,
Bid all this trash farewell;
Ye high and low, of dung and slime,
Today leave off to swell.
Subdue your pride, deny your will,
Now mortify your lust;
No share else in God's holy hill
Ye have; to hell ye must.

Norden, John. *A Progress of Piety.*
Cambridge: Cambridge University Press, 1968, pp. 77-78.

The Transitory Nature of the World

PHILIP DODDRIDGE

Spring up, my soul, with ardent flight,
Nor let this earth delude my sight,
With glittering trifles gay and vain;
Wisdom divine directs thy view,
To objects ever grand and new,
And faith displays the shining train.

Be dead, my hopes, to all below,
Nor let unbounded torrents flow,
When mourning over my withered joys;
So this deceitful world is known;
Possessed I call it not my own,
Nor glory in its painted toys.

The empty pageant rolls along;
The giddy inexperienced throng
Pursue it with enchanted eyes.
It passes in swift march away,
Still more and more its charms decay,
Till the last gaudy color dies.

My God, to Thee my soul shall turn;
For Thee my noblest passions burn,
And drink in bliss from Thee alone.
I fix on that unchanging home,
Where never-fading pleasures bloom,
Fresh springing round Thy radiant throne.

Doddridge, Philip. *The Miscellaneous Works of Philip Doddridge.*
London: Joseph Robinson, 1830, p. 1047.

Vain Amusements

JOHN NEWTON

God gives His mercies to be spent;
Your hoard will do your soul no good.
Gold is a blessing only lent,
Repaid by giving others food.

The world's esteem is but a bribe,
To buy their peace you sell your own;
The slave of a vainglorious tribe,
Who hate you while they make you known.

The joy that vain amusements give,
Oh, sad conclusion that it brings!
The honey of a crowded hive,
Defended by a thousand stings.

'Tis thus the world rewards the fools,
That live upon her treacherous smiles;
She leads them blindfold by her rules,
And ruins all whom she beguiles.

God knows the thousands who go down
From pleasure into endless woe;
And with a long despairing groan,
Blaspheme their Maker as they go.

Oh, fearful thought, be timely wise;
Delight but in a Savior's charms;
And God shall take you to the skies,
Embraced in everlasting arms.

Newton, John. *The Works of the Rev. John Newton.*
Edinburgh: Thomas Nelson, 1841, p. 543 ("Vanity of the World").

Earth Despicable, Heaven Desirable

RALPH ERSKINE

There's nothing round the spacious earth
To suit my vast desires;
To more refined and solid mirth,
My boundless thought aspires.

Fain would I leave this mournful place,
This music dull, where none
But heavy notes have any grace,
And mirth accents the moan.

Where troubles tread upon reliefs,
New woes with older blend;
Where rolling storms and circling griefs
Run round without an end.

Where waters wrestling with the stones,
Do fight themselves to foam,
And hollow clouds, with thundering groans,
Discharge their pregnant womb.

Where eagles mounting meet with rubs
That dash them from the sky;
And cedars, shrinking into shrubs,
In ruin prostrate lie.

Where sin the author of turmoils,
The cause of death and hell;
The one thing foul that all things foils,
Does most befriended dwell.

The purchaser of night and woe,
The forfeiter of day,
The debt that every man did owe,
But only God could pay.

Bewitching ill, endorsed with hope,
Subscribed with despair;
Ugly in death when eyes are ope,
Though life may paint it fair.

Small wonder that I droop alone
In such a doleful place;
When lo, my dearest Friend is gone,
My Father hides His face.

And though in words I seem to show
The fawning poets style,
Yet is my plaint no feigned woe;
I languish in exile.

I long to share the happiness
Of that triumphant throne,
That swim in seas of boundless bliss
Eternity along.

When but in drops, here by the way,
Free love distills itself,
I pour contempt on hills of prey,
And heaps of worldly pelf.

To be amid my little joys,
Thrones, scepters, crowns, and kings,
Are nothing else but little toys,
And despicable things.

Down with disdain earth's pomp I thrust,
But tempting wealth away;
Heav'n is not made of yellow dust,
Nor bliss of glittering clay.

Sweet was the hour I freedom felt
To call my Jesus mine;
To see His smiling face, and melt
In pleasures all divine.

Let fools an heaven of shades pursue,
But I for substance am;
The heaven I seek is likeness to,
And vision of the Lamb.

The worthy Lamb with glory crowned
In His august abode;
Enthroned sublime, and decked around
With all the pomp of God.

I long to join the saints above,
Who crowned with glorious bays,
Through radiant files of angels move,
And rival them in praise.

In praise to Jah, the God of love,
The fair incarnate Son,
The holy co-eternal Dove,
The good, the great Three-one.

In hope to sing without a sob
The anthem ever new,
I gladly bid the dusty globe,
And vain delights, "Adieu."

Erskine, Ralph. *Erskine's Sermons and Practical Works.*
Aberdeen: A. King & Co., 1863, VII:303-304.

A Well Secured Estate

JOHN FLAVEL

Men can't be quiet till they be assured
That their estate is good, and well-secured;
To able counsel they their deeds submit,
Entreating them with care to examine it.

Fearing some clause an enemy may wrest,
Or find a flaw; whereby he may divest
Them and their children. Oh, who can but see
How wise men in their generation be?

But do they equal cares and fears express
About their everlasting happiness?
In spiritual things 'twould grieve one's heart to see
What careless fools these careful men can be.

They act like men of common sense bereaven,
Secure their lands, and they'll trust God for heaven.
How many cases have you to submit
To lawyers' judgments? Ministers may sit

From week to week, and yet not see the face
Of one that brings a soul-concerning case.
Yea, which is worse, how seldom do you cry
To God for counsel? Or beg Him to try

Your hearts, and strictest inquisition make
Into your estate, discover your mistake?
O stupid souls, clouded with ignorance,
Is Christ and heaven no fair inheritance,

Compared with yours? Or is eternity
A shorter term than yours, that you should ply
The one so close, and totally neglect
The other, as not worth your least respect.

Perhaps the devil, whose plot from you is concealed,
Persuades your title's good, and firmly sealed
By God's own Spirit; though you never found,
One act of saving grace to lay a ground

For that persuasion. Soul, he hath thee fast,
Though he'll not let thee know it till the last;
Lord, waken sinners, make them understand,
'Twixt Thee and them, how rawly matters stand.

Give them no quiet rest until they see
Their souls secured better than lands can be.

Flavel, John. *The Works of John Flavel.*
London: The Banner of Truth Trust, 1968, V:181-182 (The Poem).

The Joy of the Lord is Your Strength

JOHN NETWON

Joy is a fruit that will not grow
In nature's barren soil;
All we can boast, till Christ we know,
Is vanity and toil.

But where the Lord has planted grace,
And made His glories known;
There fruits of heavenly joy and peace
Are found, and there alone.

A bleeding Savior, seen by faith,
A sense of pardoning love,
A hope that triumphs over death,
Give joys like those above.

To take a glimpse within the veil,
To know that God is mine,
Are springs of joy that never fail,
Unspeakable, divine!

These are the joys which satisfy,
And sanctify the mind;
Which make the spirit mount on high,
And leave the world behind.

No more, believers, mourn your lot,
But if you are the Lord's,
Resign to them that know Him not
Such joys as earth affords.

Newton, John. *The Works of the Rev. John Newton.*
Edinburgh: Thomas Nelson, 1841, p. 539.

On Jordan's Stormy Banks

DEATH

Die well,
For you cannot come back and try again.

JOHN BUNYAN

On Jordan's Stormy Banks
DEATH

"When George Gillespie was lying on his deathbed in Edinburgh, with his pillow filled with stinging apprehensions, as is often the case with God's best servants and ripest saints,...[Samuel Rutherford] writes to him: 'My reverend and dear brother, look to the east. Die well. Your life of faith is just finishing. Finish it well. Let your last act of faith be your best act. Stand not upon sanctification, but upon justification. Die on your justification not on your sanctification' ... And the dying man answered: 'There is nothing that I have done that can stand the touchstone of God's justice. Christ is all, and I am nothing.'" (Whyte, Alexander, *Samuel Rutherford and Some of his Correspondents*. Edinburgh; London: Oliphant Anderson and Ferrier, 1894.)

Look at death before it actually comes to your door. How will it go with you when you face death and the sure judgment that is to follow? Let us take our stand on the banks of the River Jordan and imagine ourselves wading across those dark waters. Visualize that, for before long we will no longer be fanciful spectators but compulsory performers in the closing acts of this drama of life and death.

Samuel Rutherford, John Bunyan, and George Gillespie knew by experience that to hold fast to Christ's bloody hand, who was cast violently by men into this river, is the only safe way to cross. Christ has triumphantly gone over and come back. He knows the fords in the icy terrifying currents of this tributary. The depths of the swollen Jordan have caused, some to go under for a moment, but Christ has never let any of His own drown. He will skillfully guide His struggling children to the stepping stones (the promises of God in Scripture). Step on them for sure footing. Knees may grow weak as conscience wisely decries, "Don't trust in your imperfect, sin-riddled obedience—a life filled with sins of commission and omission." However, His strong hand holds, steadies, and reassures the fainthearted to trust in His perfect sacrifice and obedience that have been imputed to their account. Further help is given as a glimpse is caught of the other bank where the saints of the past have prepared a grand reception and the Father is ready to welcome His precious saints.

The Promised Land

SAMUEL STENNETT

On Jordan's stormy banks I stand,
And cast a wishful eye
To Canaan's fair and happy land,
Where my possessions lie.

Oh, the transporting rapturous scene
That rises to my sight;
Sweet fields, arrayed in living green,
And rivers of delight!

There generous fruits, that never fail,
On trees immortal grow;
There rocks, and hills, and brooks, and vales,
With milk and honey flow.

All o'er those wide, extended plains
Shines one eternal day;
There God the Son forever reigns,
And scatters night away.

No chilling winds, or poisonous breath,
Can reach that healthful shore;
Sickness and sorrow, pain and death,
Are felt and feared no more.

When shall I reach that happy place,
And be forever blessed?
When shall I see my Father's face,
And in His bosom rest?

Filled with delight, my raptured soul
Can here no longer stay;
Though Jordan's waves around me roll,
Fearless I'd launch away.

Stennett, Samuel. *The Works of Samuel Stennett, D.D.*
London: Printed for Thomas Tegg, 1824, pp. 554-555.

Time How Short

JOHN NEWTON

Time, with an unwearied hand,
Pushes round the seasons past;
And in life's frail glass, the sand
Sinks apace, not long to last;
Many as well as you or I,
Who last year assembled thus,
In their silent graves now lie;
Graves will open soon for us.

Daily sin and care and strife,
While the Lord prolongs our breath,
Make it but a dying life,
Or a kind of living death;
Wretched they, and most forlorn,
Who no better portion know;
Better never to have been born
Than to have our all below.

When constrained to go alone,
Leaving all you love behind,
Entering on a world unknown,
What will then support your mind?
When the Lord His summons sends,
Earthly comforts lose their power;
Honor, riches, kindred, friends,
Cannot cheer a dying hour.

Happy souls, who fear the Lord,
Time is not too swift for you;
When your Savior gives the word,
Glad you'll bid the world adieu.
Then He'll wipe away your tears,
Near Himself appoint your place;
Swifter fly, ye rolling years,
Lord, we long to see Thy face.

Newton, John. *The Works of the Rev. John Newton.*
Edinburgh: Thomas Nelson, 1841, pp. 572-573.

Death

GEORGE HERBERT

Death, thou was once an uncouth, hideous thing,
Nothing but bones;
The sad effect of sadder groans;
Thy mouth was open, but thou could not sing.

For we considered thee as at some six
Or ten years hence,
After the loss of life and sense,
Flesh being turned to dust, and bones to sticks.

We looked on this side of thee, shooting short,
Where we did find
The shells of fledge souls left behind,
Dry dust, which sheds no tears, but may extort.

But since our Savior's death did put some blood
Into thy face,
Thou art grown fair and full of grace,
Much in request, much sought for, as a good.

For we do now behold thee gay and glad,
As at doomsday,
When souls shall wear their new array,
And all thy bones with beauty shall be clad.

Therefore we can go die as sleep, and trust
Half that we have
Unto honest faithful grave,
Making our pillows either down or dust.

Herbert, George. *The Works of George Herbert in Prose and Verse.*
London: Bell and Daldy, 1859, II:213-214.

When Shall I Be at Ease?

OLIVER HEYWOOD

When shall my dunghill body give release
Unto my sad imprisoned soul that lies
Thus caged in darkness? When shall I have ease
From all my sorrows and iniquities?
When shall I cease to sin, begin to praise,
Leave my complaints with this unhappy world?
When shall I see my blessed Redeemer's face,
Whose heart rejoicing words have me extolled?

Sometimes methinks I feel but the firstfruits
Of Canaan's fruitful heart rejoicing land,
Which with such pleasing sweetness me recruits,
As makes my fainting heart admiring stand.
Lord, think I then, when shall my soul enjoy
That happy state of which I have a glance;
When will my God this house of clay destroy,
That to Thy glory my soul might advance?

How long shall this my dead, sad, carnal heart
Within my pained, pinning bosom lie?
How long shall Satan catch me with his art
And lead me captive with proud victory?
When shall my heaven-born soul mount up and sing
Among those naked souls the angels' ditties,
Whose heart delighting tune make heaven's ring
With hallelujahs in the imperial city.

Ah, woe is me who sojourn like a stranger
In these rude tents of Meshech here below!
Must Kedar keep my soul in doleful danger
To be massacred by each deadly foe?
Ah, woeful time of banishment from home!
Must I an exile live from my dear Father?
O Absalom, my case is now become
As thine; my God and I must be together!

Oh, with what breathings doth my soul aspire
Like low Zaccheus in a lofty tree!
So by Thine ordinances I desire
To see Thee, taste Thee, and to be with Thee.
Sometimes I bless Thee; Thou dost me afford
A gracious smile and turn to me again;
Sometimes I hear a heart-reviving word
Fetch me to life and lenify my pain.

"Lord, it is good to be here," then I cry,
Thus would I live, here let me dwell for aye;
Mistaking earth for heaven and my joy,
Which is at home for comforts in my way.
But then, alas, my soul doth sadly feel
A dark eclipse and want of those sweet rays,
Which did me warm, and thus I madly reel
To all extremes, and thus I spend my days,
Thus shall I end my days!

Heywood, Oliver. *The Rev. Oliver Heywood, B.A. His Autobiography, Diaries, Anecdote and Event Books in Three Volumes.* Brighouse: A. B. Bayes, 1882, I:130-131.

The Blessing of Hope in Death

SAMUEL DAVIES

Yes, I must bow my head and die;
What then can bear my spirit up?
In nature's last extremity,
Who can afford one ray of hope?

Then all created comforts fail,
And earth speaks nothing but despair;
And you, my friends, must bid farewell,
And leave your fellow-traveller.

Yet, Savior, Thine almighty power
Even then can sure support afford,
Even then that hope shall smile secure,
That's now supported by Thy Word.

Searcher of hearts, oh, try me now,
Nor let me build upon the sand;
Oh, teach me now myself to know,
That I may then the trial stand.

Davies, Samuel. *Collected Poems of Samuel Davies.*
Gainsville: Scholars' Facsimiles & Reprints, 1968, p. 173.

The Great Journey

PHILIP DODDRIDGE

Behold the path that mortals tread
Down to the regions of the dead;
Nor will the fleeting moments stay,
Nor can we measure back our way.

Our kindred and our friends are gone;
Know, O my soul, this doom thy own;
Feeble as theirs my mortal frame,
The same my way, my house the same.

From vital air, from cheerful light,
To the cold grave's perpetual night,
From scenes of duty, means of grace,
Must I to God's tribunal pass.

Important journey, awful view,
How great the change, the scenes how new;
The golden gates of heaven displayed,
Or hell's fierce flames and gloomy shade.

Awake, my soul, thy way prepare,
And lose in this each mortal care;
With steady feet that path be trod,
Which through the grave conducts to God.

Jesus, to Thee my all I trust,
And, if Thou call me down to dust,
I know Thy voice, I bless Thy hand,
And die in smiles at Thy command.

What was my terror is my joy;
These views my brightest hopes employ,
To go, 'ere many years are o'er,
Secure I shall return no more.

Doddridge, Philip. *The Miscellaneous Works of Philip Doddridge.*
London: Joseph Ogle Robinson, 1830, pp. 987-988.

Death–Dreadful or Delightful

ISAAC WATTS

Death—'tis a melancholy day
To those that have no God,
When the poor soul is forced away
To seek her last abode.

In vain to heaven she lifts her eyes,
But guilt, a heavy chain,
Still drags her downward from the skies
To darkness, fire, and pain.

Awake and mourn, ye heirs of hell,
Let stubborn sinners fear;
You must be driven from earth and dwell
A long forever there.

See how the pit gapes wide for you,
And flashes in your face;
And thou, my soul, look downward too,
And sing recovering grace.

He is a God of sovereign love
That promised heaven to me,
And taught my thoughts to soar above,
Where happy spirits be.

Prepare me, Lord, for Thy right hand,
Then come the joyful day;
Come, death, and some celestial band,
To bear my soul away.

Watts, Isaac. *The Psalms and Hymns of Isaac Watts.*
Morgan: Soli Deo Gloria Publications, 1997, p. 438.

It's Reckoning Day

EDWARD TAYLOR

Look till thy looks look wan, my soul; here's ground
The world's bright eye's dashed out. Daylight so brave
Benighted; the sparkling sun, paled round
With flouring rays, lies buried in its grave;
The candle of the world blown out, down fell
Life knocked ahead by death, heaven by hell.

Alas, this world all filled up to the brim
With sins, deaths, devils, crowding men to hell;
For whose relief God's milk-white Lamb stepped in,
Whom those crust imps did worry, flesh and fell;
Tread under foot, did clap their wings and so
Like dunghill cocks over their conquered crow.

Brave, pious fraud, as if the setting sun
Dropped like a ball of fire into the seas,
And so went out; but to the east come run.
You'll meet the morn shrined with its flowering rays.
This Lamb in laying of these lions dead,
Drank of the brook, and so lift up His head.

Oh, sweet, sweet joy! These rampant fiends be fooled;
They made their gall his winding sheet, although
They of the heartache die must, or be cooled
With inflammation of the lungs, they know.
He's cancelling the bond, and making pay,
And balancing accounts—its reckoning day.

See, how He from the counthouse shining went
In flashing folds of burnished glory, and
Dashed out all curses from the covenant;
Hath justices acquittance in His hand;
Plucked out death's sting; the serpent's head did maul;
The bars and gates of hell, He brake down all.

Taylor, Edward. *Poetical Works of Edward Taylor.*
Princeton: Princeton Press, 1943, p. 133.

The Song of Triumph over Death and the Grave

RALPH ERSKINE

Faith sings although the body dies,
The promise is enjoyed;
This mortal shall immortal rise,
And death shall be destroyed.

Where is thy killing sting, O death,
Addicted to devour?
Through grace we now despise thy wrath,
And we defy thy power.

O grave, where is thy victory?
The bolted prison, where?
Our king victorious conquered thee,
And we the conquest share.

The sting of death is sin indeed,
The strength of sin the law;
But thence our law-fulfilling Head
Did sting and strength withdraw.

Thanks to the God of victory,
Who makes us this, by faith,
In Christ, our living Head on high,
Triumphant over death.

Then steadfast may our hearts remain,
And in His work abound;
Through whom our labors not in vain,
With such an issue crowned.

Erskine, Ralph. *Erskine's Sermons and Practical Works.*
Aberdeen: A. King & Co., 1863, VII:613.

Children Dying in the Arms of Jesus
SAMUEL STENNETT

Thy life I read, my dearest Lord,
With transport all divine;
Thine image trace in every Word,
Thy love in every line.

Methinks I see a thousand charms
Spread over Thy lovely face,
While infants in Thy tender arms
Receive the smiling grace.

"I take these little lambs," said He,
"And lay them in My breast;
Protection they shall find in Me,
In Me be ever blessed."

"Death may the band of life unloose,
But can't dissolve My love;
Millions of infant souls compose
The family above.

"Their feeble frames My power shall raise,
And mold with heavenly skill;
I'll give them tongues to sing My praise,
And hands to do My will."

His words the happy parents hear,
And shout with joys divine,
"Dear Savior, all we have and are
Shall be forever Thine."

Stennett, Samuel. *The Works of Samuel Stennett, D.D.*
London: Thomas Tegg, 1824, p. 553.

Christ's Presence Makes Death Easy

ISAAC WATTS

Why should we start and fear to die?
What timorous worms we mortals are;
Death is the gate of endless joy,
And yet we dread to enter there.

The pains, the groans, and dying strife,
Fright our approaching souls away;
Still we shrink back again to life,
Fond of our prison and our clay.

Oh, if my Lord would come and meet,
My soul should stretch her wings in haste,
Fly fearless through death's iron gate,
Nor feel the terrors as she passed.

Jesus can make a dying bed
Feel soft as downy pillows are,
While on His breast I lean my head,
And breathe my life out sweetly there.

Watts, Isaac. *The Psalms and Hymns of Isaac Watts.*
Morgan: Soli Deo Gloria Publications, 1997, p. 424.

Face to Face

HEAVEN

They shall see His face,
And His name shall be on their foreheads.
There shall be no night there;
They need no lamp nor light of the sun,
For the Lord God gives them light.
And they shall reign forever and ever.

REVELATION 22:4-5

Face to Face
HEAVEN

As our minds are informed by the Scriptures and the Holy Spirit of the excellency and desirability of Christ, our affections are seized. Our desires are cast upon Christ for "if we had it all absolutely secured to us that this world is still promising, it would not come within a thousand miles of satisfying our hearts. Whether the hopes of our hearts are to be fulfilled within the veil or no, that remains to be seen; but all the things without the veil taken together do not any longer even pretend to promise a hope to hearts like ours. Our Forerunner has carried away our hearts with Him. We have no heart left for any one but Him, or anything without or within the veil that He is not and is not in." (Whyte, Alexander. *Bunyan's Characters, Third Series, The Holy War,* Edinburgh; London: Oliphant Anderson and Ferrier, 1902, pp. 177-178.)

Pilgrims and strangers we are in this alien land as we journey to heaven. And though the country we are passing through has its enjoyments, and many times various trials and hardships, our longings, our hopes, our eyes are all steadfastly set on our celestial home. The Holy Spirit has given us affections that are irresistibly drawn to and bound by cords of love to Christ. The Lover of our souls has carried away our hearts and holds them captive in heaven.

Since we were made for Jesus, our deepest desires can never be satisfied without the veil. Only within the veil, when we finally arrive home, shall our weary souls find rest. Here there is joy full of glory. Here there is satisfaction eternal and complete. Here shall pierced hearts be healed. Here there are myriads and myriads of voices in endless praise of the wonder of heaven. Here at last we shall behold the Captor of our hearts face to face.

The Covenant and Confidence of Faith

RICHARD BAXTER

Lord, it belongs not to my care
Whether I die or live;
To love and serve Thee is my share,
And this Thy grace must give.

If life be long, I will be glad,
That I may long obey;
If short, yet why should I be sad
To welcome endless day?

Christ leads me through no darker rooms
Than He went through before;
He that unto God's kingdom comes
Must enter by this door.

Come, Lord, when grace hath made me meet
Thy blessed face to see;
For if Thy work on earth be sweet,
What will Thy glory be!

My knowledge of that life is small,
The eye of faith is dim;
But 'tis enough that Christ knows all,
And I shall be with Him.

Baxter, Richard. *Poetical Fragments by Richard Baxter.*
W. Germany: Gregg International Publishers Limited, 1971, pp. 82-83.

The Arrival

AUGUSTUS TOPLADY

Hearken, the Savior's voice at last
Invites His sufferer home,
And tells thee all thy toil is past,
But thy reward is come.

Till meet for bliss on earth detained,
The conquest Thou hast won;
Through much temptation thou hast gained,
The prize, and reached the crown.

While shouting angels chant their joys,
And tune their notes the higher,
And clap their wings, for, oh, thy voice,
Is added to the choir.

Of his inheritance above,
They hail a saint possessed;
Made meet, by his Redeemer's love,
To be Jehovah's guest.

Swift as an arrow through the air,
The towering spirit flies,
Entrusted to a seraph's care,
And convoyed to the skies.

On the expanded wings of love,
He seeks his high abode,
To meet the happy souls above,
That are brought home to God.

Him they salute with lifted cry,
As soon as entered there,
"But for Thy favored ministry,
Or we had not been here.

"From pain to glory summoned forth,
Thrice welcome from below,
Our fellow-sufferer on earth,
Our fellow angel now!"

While humbly he draws near the throne,
The Savior's crystal seat;
Gives Him the praise, and casts his crown
At His redeeming feet.

Lifted above the reach of pain,
We soon shall change our place;
And join Emmanuel's shining train,
And see His blissful face.

Rejoicing in that glorious hope,
We bear His cross below;
We quickly shall be taken up,
Sublimer joys to know.

For our arrival into bliss,
Our friends in glory wait;
Cut short Thy work in righteousness,
And make their joys complete!

The happy soul whom Jesus gives
In Him to live and die;
Its blessed transition scarce perceives
Into eternity.

A sight of Him that conquered death,
In our last moments given,
Shall elevate our languid faith,
And charm us into heaven.

Christ when expiring Stephen viewed,
He scorned death's utmost power,
And calmly fell asleep in God,
Amid the stony shower.

Assist us, Lord, to walk and live,
In Zion's heavenly road,
And then our souls to Thee receive,
When called to meet our God.

A little while, and we shall soar
To yonder promised land,
And meet our brethren gone before,
Enthroned at Thy right hand.

Thy praise shall actuate each tongue,
Thy love our hearts inflame;
And we with them shall sing the song
Of Moses and the Lamb.

Toplady, Augustus. *The Works of Augustus Toplady.*
London: J. Chidley, 1837, pp. 904-905
(Genesis 5:24, "And Enoch walked with God, he was not, for God took him").

A Song of Praise for the Hope of Glory
JOHN MASON

I sojourn in a vale of tears;
Alas, how can I sing?
My harp doth on the willows hang,
Distuned in every string.
My music is a captive's chains,
Harsh sounds my ears do fill;
How shall I sing sweet Zion's song
On this side Zion's hill?

Yet lo, I hear a joyful sound,
"Surely I quickly come";
Each word much sweetness doth distill,
Like a full honeycomb.

And dost Thou come, my dearest Lord?
And dost Thou surely come?
And dost Thou surely quickly come?
Methinks I am at home.

Come then, my dearest, dearest Lord,
My sweetest, surest Friend;
Come, for I loathe these Kedar tents,
Thy fiery chariots send.
What have I here? My thoughts and joys
Are all packed up and gone;
My eager soul would follow them
To Thine eternal throne.

What have I in this barren land?
My Jesus is not here;
Mine eyes will never be blessed until
My Jesus doth appear.
My Jesus is gone up to heaven,
To get a place for me;
For 'tis His will that where He is,
There should His servants be.

Canaan I view from Pisgah's top,
Of Canaan's grapes I taste;
My Lord, who sends unto me here,
Will send for me at last.
I have a God that changes not,
Why should I be perplexed?
My God, that owns me in this world,
Will own me in the next.

Go fearless, then, my soul, with God,
Into another room;
Thou, who hast walked with Him here,
Go see Thy God at home.

View death with a believing eye,
It has an angel's face;
And this kind angel will prefer
Thee to an angel's place.

The grave is but a fining pot
Unto believing eyes;
For there the flesh shall lose its dross,
And like the sun shall rise.
The world, which I have known too well,
Hath mocked me with its lies;
How gladly could I leave behind
Its vexing vanities?

My dearest friends they dwell above,
Them will I go to see;
And all my friends in Christ below
Will soon come after me.
Fear not the trump's earth-rending sound,
Dread not the day of doom;
For He, that is to be thy Judge,
Thy Savior is become.

Blessed be my God that gives me light,
Who in the dark did grope;
Blessed be my God, the God of love,
Who causes me to hope.
Here's the Word's signet, comfort's staff,
And here is grace's chain;
By these Thy pledges, Lord, I know
My hopes are not in vain.

Mason, John. *Spiritual Songs, or Songs of Praise to Almighty God.*
Edinburgh: James Taylor, 1880, pp. 89-93.

Anthems for the Cathedral of Exeter

JOSEPH HALL

Leave, O my soul, this baser world below,
Oh, leave this doleful dungeon of woe;
And soar aloft to that supernal rest,
That makes all the saints and angels blessed.
Lo, there the Godhead's radiant throne,
Like to ten thousand suns in one!

Lo, there thy Savior dear in glory dight
Adored of all the powers of heavens bright;
Lo, where that head, that bled with thorny wound,
Shine ever with celestial honor crowned;
That hand, that held the scornful reed,
Makes all the fiends infernal dread.

That back and side, that ran with bloody streams,
Daunt angels' eyes with their majestic beams;
Those feet, once fastened to the cursed tree,
Trample on death and hell, in glorious glee.
Those lips, once drenched with gall, do make
With their dread doom the world to quake.

Behold those joys thou never canst behold,
Those precious gates of pearl, those streets of gold,
Those streams of life, those trees of paradise,
That never can be seen by mortal eyes;
And when thou seest this state divine,
Think that it is or shall be thine.

See there the happy troops of purest sprights,
That live above in endless true delights;
And see where once thyself shall ranged be,
And look and long for immortality;
And now, beforehand, help to sing
Hallelujahs to heaven's King.

Hall, Joseph. *The Works of the Right Reverend Father in God, Joseph Hall.*
London: C. Whittingham, 1808, p. 274.

A Longing for Heaven

WILLIAM BURKITT

Jerusalem, my happy home,
When shall I come to thee?
When shall my labors have an end;
Thy joys when shall we see?

Thy gates are richly set with pearls,
Most glorious to behold;
Thy walls are all of precious stone,
Thy streets are paved with gold.

Thy gardens and thy pleasant fruits
Continually are green;
So sweet a sight by human eye
Has never yet been seen.

If heaven be thus glorious, Lord,
Why must I keep from thence?
What folly is it that makes me loth
To die and go from hence?

Reach down, reach down Thine arm of grace,
And cause me to ascend,
Where congregations ne'er break up,
And Sabbaths have no end.

When wilt Thou come to me, Oh Lord?
Oh come, my Lord, most dear!
Come nearer, nearer, nearer still;
I'm well when Thou art near.

My dear Redeemer is above,
Him will I go to see;
And all my friends in Christ below
Shall soon come after me.

Jerusalem, my happy home,
Oh, how I long for thee!
Then shall my labors have an end,
When once thy joys I see.

Burkitt, William. *An Help and Guide to Christian Families.*
London: Longman, Hurst, and Co. and J. Mawman, 1822, pp. 147-148.

I Am a Debtor

ROBERT MURRAY McCHEYNE

When this passing world is done,
When has sunk yon glaring sun,
When we stand with Christ in glory,
Looking o'er life's finished story,
Then, Lord, shall I fully know—
Not till then—how much I owe.

When I hear the wicked call,
On the rocks and hills to fall;
When I see them start and shrink,
On the fiery deluge brink.
Then, Lord, shall I fully know—
Not till then—how much I owe.

When I stand before the throne,
Dressed in beauty not my own;
When I see Thee as Thou art,
Love Thee with unsinning heart.
Then, Lord, shall I fully know—
Not till then—how much I owe.

When the praise of heaven I hear,
Loud as thunders to the ear,
Loud as many waters' noise,

Sweet as harp's melodious voice.
Then, Lord, shall I fully know—
Not till then—how much I owe.

Even on earth, as through a glass
Darkly, let Thy glory pass;
Make forgiveness feel so sweet,
Make Thy Spirit's help so meet,
Even on earth, Lord, make me know
Something of how much I owe.

Chosen not for good in me,
Wakened up from wrath to flee,
Hidden in the Savior's side,
By the Spirit sanctified;
Teach me, Lord, on earth to show,
By my love, how much I owe.

Oft I walk beneath the cloud,
Dark as midnight's gloomy shroud;
But, when fear is at the height,
Jesus comes, and all is light.
Blessed Jesus, bid me show,
Doubting saints how much I owe.

When in flowery paths I tread,
Oft by sin I'm captive led;
Oft I fall, but still arise;
The Spirit comes, the tempter flies.
Blessed Spirit, bid me show
Weary sinners all I owe.

Oft the nights of sorrow reign—
Weeping, sickness, sighing, pain;
But a night Thine anger burns;
Morning comes and joy returns.
God of comforts, bid me show
To Thy poor, how much I owe.

McCheyne, Robert Murray. *The Life and Remains, Letters, Lectures, and Poems
of the Rev. Robert Murray McCheyne*, edited by Rev. Andrew A. Bonar,
Robert Carter, NY, 1873, pp. 350-351.

There the Weary Are at Rest

JOHN NEWTON

Courage, my soul, behold the prize
The Savior's love provides—
Eternal life beyond the skies
For all whom here He guides.

The wicked cease from troubling there,
The weary are at rest;
Sorrow, and sin, and pain, and care,
No more approach the blessed.

A wicked world, and wicked heart,
With Satan now are joined;
Each acts a too successful part
In harassing my mind.

In conflict with this threefold troop,
How weary, Lord, am I!
Did not Thy promise bear me up,
My soul must faint and die.

But fighting in my Savior's strength,
Though mighty are my foes,
I shall a conqueror be at length
Over all that can oppose.

Then why, my soul, complain or fear?
The crown of glory see!
The more I toil and suffer here,
The sweeter rest will be.

Newton, John. *The Works of the Rev. John Newton.*
Edinburgh: Thomas Nelson, 1841, p. 595.

Glory Which Delights Beholder's Eyes

JOHN FLAVEL

Bare seeds have no great beauty, but, inhumed,
That which they had is lost and quite consumed;
They soon corrupt and grow more base, by odds,
When dead and buried underneath the clods.

It falls in baseness, but at length doth rise
In glory which delights beholders' eyes.
How great a difference have a few days made,
Between it in the bushel and the blade!

This lovely, lively emblem aptly may
Type out the glorious resurrection day;
Wherein the saints that in the dust do lie,
Shall rise in glory, vigor, dignity.

With singing, in that morning they arise,
And dazzle glory, such as mortal eyes
Never viewed on earth. The sparkling beauties here,
No more can equalize their splendor there,

Than glimmering glowworms do the fairest star
That shines in heaven, or the stones that are
In every street, may competition hold
With glittering diamonds in rings of gold.

For unto Christ's most glorious body they
Shall be conformed in glory at that day;
Whose luster would, should it on mortals fall,
Transport a Stephen, and confound a Paul.

'Tis now a coarse and crazy house of clay;
But, oh, how dear do souls for lodgings pay!
Few more than I; for thou, my soul, hast been
Within these tents of Kedar cooped in.

Where, with distempers clogged, thou make thy moans,
And, for deliverance, with tears and groans
Hast often sued; cheer up, the time will be
When thou from all these troubles shall be free.

No jarring humors, cloudy vapors, rheums,
Pains, aches, or whatever else consumes
My day in grief; while in the Christian race,
Flesh lags behind, and can't keep equal pace

With the more willing spirit. None of these
Shall thenceforth clog thee or disturb thine ease.

Flavel, John. *The Works of John Flavel.*
London: The Banner of Truth Trust, 1968, V:94 (The Poem).

Author Index

Title Index